The Way of Power

A Series of Lectures Delivered before the Japan Convention for Deepening of Spiritual Life, at Karuizawa, Stenographically Reported

by

John Paul

First Fruits Press
Wilmore, Kentucky
c2015

The Way of Power: a series of lectures delivered before the Japan Convention for Deepening of Spiritual Life, at Karuizawa, stenographically reported by John Paul.

First Fruits Press, ©2015
Previously published: New York and London : Fleming H. Revell, Company, ©1918.

ISBN: 9781621712282 (print), 9781621712299 (digital), 9781621712305 (kindle)

Digital version at http://place.asburyseminary.edu/firstfruitsheritagematerial/102/

First Fruits Press is a digital imprint of the Asbury Theological Seminary, B.L. Fisher Library. Asbury Theological Seminary is the legal owner of the material previously published by the Pentecostal Publishing Co. and reserves the right to release new editions of this material as well as new material produced by Asbury Theological Seminary. Its publications are available for noncommercial and educational uses, such as research, teaching and private study. First Fruits Press has licensed the digital version of this work under the Creative Commons Attribution Noncommercial 3.0 United States License. To view a copy of this license, visit http://creativecommons.org/licenses/by-nc/3.0/us/.

For all other uses, contact:

First Fruits Press
B.L. Fisher Library
Asbury Theological Seminary
204 N. Lexington Ave.
Wilmore, KY 40390
http://place.asburyseminary.edu/firstfruits

Paul, John, 1877-1967.
   The way of power : a series of lectures delivered before the Japan Convention for Deepening of Spiritual Life, at Karuizawa / stenographically reported by John Paul.
   190 pages ; 21 cm.
   Wilmore, Ky. : First Fruits Press, ©2015.
   Reprint. Previously published: New York ; London : Fleming H. Revell Company, ©1918.
   ISBN: 9781621712282 (pbk.)
   1. Holiness. 2. Spiritual life. I. Title. II. Convention for Deepening of Spiritual Life (Karuizawa, Japan)
BV4501 .P38 2015   204

Cover design by Wesley Wilcox

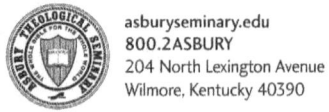

First Fruits Press
The Academic Open Press of Asbury Theological Seminary
204 N. Lexington Ave., Wilmore, KY 40390
859-858-2236
first.fruits@asburyseminary.edu
asbury.to/firstfruits

The Way of Power

The Way of Power

*A Series of Lectures Delivered before the Japan
Convention for Deepening of Spiritual Life,
at Karuizawa, Stenographically Reported*

BY

JOHN PAUL
*Vice-President, Asbury College
Wilmore, Ky.*

NEW YORK   CHICAGO
Fleming H. Revell Company
LONDON   AND   EDINBURGH

Copyright, 1918, by
FLEMING H. REVELL COMPANY

New York : 158 Fifth Avenue
Chicago: 17 North Wabash Ave.
London : 21 Paternoster Square
Edinburgh : 75 Princes Street

PREFACE

THE public will pardon the artistic deficiencies in the composition of these addresses, and we trust that an apology will not be necessary for the fact that they were delivered extemporaneously, since they follow a well defined line of thought. If we understand the mind of the average man, he is more interested in a thing of life than a thing of art. The jagged methods of emphasis, rendered perhaps a little more jagged by the vicissitudes of a stenographic report, might be entirely smoothed out if the author were to re-write these lectures in composition form; and the arguments imbedded therein might be more clearly articulated; but they would lose something which they are bound to have derived from the associations of a convention which in denominational complexion and spiritual passion could hardly be duplicated in the Christian world.

It may add a mental setting to the thoughts of the serious reader to remind him that the best intellect and the best devotion of every widely known Christian denomination, with the possible exception of the Roman Catholic, was represented in the audience that received these lectures, and that the meetings resulted in much definite blessing; so much that many of the written testimonies have been published, of people who took higher ground in the Karuizawa Convention.

It was in deference to the judgment of certain Christian leaders that these messages were reported for publication. This was recommended because doctrinally they are representative of one of the standard interpretations of a theme in which all Christendom is acquiring an increased interest; because, while the interpretation of Christian holiness as here presented has borne much good fruit, since the days of John Wesley, the presentation of it in these addresses is "characterized by breadth of vision, charity and tolerance, without sacrificing those qualities of clearness and aggressiveness which are appreciated by candid men of all schools."

Wilmore, Ky. J. P.

These lectures, translated by M. Matsumoto, Acting President Kwansei Gakuin, Kobe, are published in Japanese by The Christian Literature Society, Tokyo, Japan.

CONTENTS

LECTURE   PAGE

I. EMPTIED AND FILLED. 1 John.

Why the church needs the blessing. Variegated light. John's burden for the church. Ways and means of happiness. A heavy indictment. Deeper experiences cannot precede intelligence. The fulness that fills....   9

II. THE OBJECT OF POWER. Acts 1:5, 8.

Personal salvation completed. Discovering our limitations. The majesty of power. The higher force. In touch with facts. Unanswerable arguments. The undying testimony. Exalting Jesus....................   26

III. THE FAREWELL SOLICITUDE OF JESUS. John 17.

A double preservation. Not of the world. Through the truth. For the winners and the won. Knowledge is experience. The world's greatest lesson. "Behold my glory." For a world-wide revival. Singleness of heart. The far-reaching remedy.....................   46

IV. PURSUIT AND POSSESSION. 1 Cor. 12 and 13.

A sure evidence of life. Be saved from ambiguous terms. What Paul showed them. Take the mean between the extremes. Prevents the shipwreck of sound ideals. Possession sublimer than pursuit. A word to timid souls...................................   68

CONTENTS

LECTURE / PAGE

V. SEE YOURSELF FIRST. Isaiah 6.
Heart language the same in every age. The contagious properties of grace. A pioneer in Bible holiness. Deep answereth unto deep. When the seer saw himself. Responding to a conviction. Isaiah's new theology. When earthquakes form continents. Man's extremity. The candle of the Lord.............. 85

VI. THE GREAT TRANSACTION. Romans 12.
To be and to do. A standard consciously chosen. Sufferers and saints. Our own spirit bears witness. Heart service greater than skilled service. The more excellent consecration. Our part may be understood. "Prove me, saith the Lord." The challenge. Guard the offering and pray.............. 104

VII. THE VICARIOUS TRAGEDY. John 3:16.
A life laid down. Right is right forever. Adam's imitators. What wondrous love. Two parties to the transaction. Consistent tears. The vision and the burden........ 124

VIII. "MY CUP." Psalm 23.
Soul sickness. The progeny of Satan. Heaven's overtures. Falling short without falling. Quarrelling with symbols. Blessings that flow. Saved from the fog. Looking for stage four............................... 141

IX. SOUL PILOTS. Hebrews 12.
Following our hearts. The Wesleyan formula. A proof of the Father's love. A four-cornered fact. The issue all must face. When the chastening ceases.............. 159

X. VICTORY. Genesis 32.
God did not evolve. "God Almighty appeared unto me." A lesson in the valley. Arriving at "number one." A passion to be made whole. Incorporate the blessing. Our doctrinal growing point. Multiplying a man. The evening halo....................... 173

I

EMPTIED AND FILLED

BASED ON THE FIRST EPISTLE OF JOHN

"These things write we unto you that your joy may be full."—1 Jno. 1:4.

THE task of evangelizing the world is in the hands of the Church rather than in the hands of the ordained ministry. When Jesus said, "Ye are the salt of the earth," He did not say this to the overseers of the flock, to the pastors or elders alone; it was true of them because they were a part of the Church of Christ. When He said, "Ye are the light of the world," He meant all of His servants had this trust of reflecting His light to the world.

First of all, the field of the ministry is the Church; and ultimately the Church is God's commissioned agency to the world. We have acted as if we believed otherwise in many centers of Christianity. Some of us can remember the time when it seemed to be the task of the ministry exclusively to evangelize the world. The Church, the laity, the men and women of the Church, did not seem to feel that a very great burden of responsibility rested upon them. They sometimes felt they ought to contribute and help the preacher that he might engage in the great world conflict, but it has only been in recent times that the Church has begun to see that it shared equally with the ministry the task of evangelizing the world. But when we become fully awakened to this truth, there falls upon the ministry a burden of responsibility to look after the spiritual life of the Church, in order that it may be equal to the responsibility of evangelizing the world; and as this very simple philosophy becomes more apparent to the ministry, there comes with it an increased burden upon the heart of the ministry for the full salvation of the Church, as the hope of evangelizing the world. As we see this fact more clearly, we who are in the ministry must feel with increasing concern that there can be no success commensurate with our task of evangelizing the world until we can have greater success in deepening the spiritual life of the Church.

Why the Church Needs the Blessing

The greatest evangelists, they who feel that their mission is to the unbelieving world, the evangelists who move the largest communities, can only count their converts by thousands; and it is very rare that you find a man with such Sinai truth in his preaching and such magnetism in his personality that we can number his converts by thousands; but when we can, he has barely touched the edge of the great problem of world evangelism. World evangelism is not to come through oral arguments and eloquent appeals from the pulpit. I am not reflecting upon the work of such evangelists; they have their place, and they have an inspirational value; but world evangelism is to come through the people of God as a whole; they are the salt of the earth; they are the light of the world, and when they become so delivered from sin and filled with Christ's sentiments and His life, when men take knowledge of them that they have been with Jesus, they will begin to solve this problem. Unless they take knowledge of us that we have been with Jesus, it will profit but little for them to discover that we have been to college or that we are sound in doctrine. World evangelism as a human problem is too great to be solved. It is not a problem of evolution, nor is it a problem of education or human ingenuity. It is a problem whose solution God assumes; but He has only one way of solving this problem, that is, through you and me and all His people, regardless of our intellectual calibre, or what may be our position in the Church of Christ.

Now, with this before us, do we permit ourselves to become burdened for the sanctification of the Church, that it might be "meet for the Master's use," that the church might be "filled with all the fulness of God," that it might be so blessed as to be a blessing? John the Beloved was impressed with this situation we have tried to outline, and he addressed his message in this first epistle, not to the unbelieving world, but to the people of God, in the hope of impressing them with the necessity of full salvation.

Variegated Light

In our statements during this convention, we shall recognize that there are several ways of apprehending the deeper life, entirely in harmony with the Scriptures and with each other, which may seem to contradict each other, if examined superficially. We shall be at liberty to use any term that seems convenient, with reference to the deepening of the spiritual life, duly considering those present who entertain technical differences, so long as they agree with our object. The only class for which I fear, is the class who believe there is no such a thing as a deeper life, and who therefore cannot be brought to long for a deeper life. We are not discouraged with that class who feel in their hearts a deep desire for better things in the spiritual life, even though they may differ with us. Our point of agreement has tremendous pre-eminence. So long as a man has an appetite and is full of hunger for spiritual things, we can find a way around the intellectual difficulties.

EMPTIED AND FILLED

We can and must get together on one thing, namely, that we are hungering and thirsting. All of the expressions by which we seek to convey our thoughts are subject to human limitations and are often insufficient to give the full meaning of divine truth. The Master at one time said to his disciples, "I have many things to say unto you, but ye cannot bear them now." I shall pay you the compliment of not adhering to that in these services, but of stating to you frankly and fully the message that I have for you as we study the Scriptures, feeling that you are far enough advanced to bear the few things I am able to say, and much more. I shall hold you to a contract to take part in the studies of this convention, and only to accept the words spoken as you confirm them by the Scripture; and you are requested to pray for the one that speaks to you. Like the fisherman when he drew the net of good and bad fish out of the sea, you are asked to put the good into vessels and cast the bad away.

John's Burden for the Church

The first Epistle General of John is addressed to all Christians, including the group in this audience today. In his opening words, the apostle impresses us with his familiarity with the great theme upon which he is about to launch. He says that he presents it to us with a special object: "That which we have seen and heard declare we unto you, that ye also may have fellowship with us." He seemed to say to his audience, We occupy a plane which we hereby invite you to occupy with us, and these things are written in order to give you a lift in that direction. The plane that he occupies is indicated in the words, "Our fellowship is with the Father and with His Son, Jesus Christ." His special object is otherwise stated when he says, "These things write we unto you that your joy may be full." We gather from that, that he gets his fulness of joy out of the fellowship to which he has just referred; fellowship with the Father and with His Son, Jesus Christ. This then is the message which he proposes to elaborate in order to get results: "The message which we have heard of him and declare unto you, that God is light and in him is no darkness at all." Then, speaking of the subject of fellowship again, he says: "If we say that we have *fellowship* with him and walk in darkness, we lie and do not the truth." And again, "If we walk in the light as he is in the light, we have *fellowship* one with another; and the blood of Jesus Christ his Son cleanseth us from all sin." This latter is a very clear statement which needs no comment in order to make it plain, and needs no defense in order to keep it from being explained away. It is an unshakable doctrinal point which is due to be kept in mind as representing a fundamental element, wherever one would lay emphasis upon the fulness of the blessing of the Gospel of Christ.

There were some in St. John's audience, it would seem, who did not accept such a statement as this, and who were not in an attitude of humility and open-heartedness; but who, instead of going to the extreme of confessing themselves incurably sinful, as many do today, went to the extreme of self-sufficiency, claiming to have all the deliverance they needed. They were under some kind of delusion which made it impossible for the doctrine or the experience of cleansing through the blood of Christ to reach them. So John injects this statement: "If we say that we have no sin, we deceive ourselves, and the truth is not in us. If we confess our sins, he is faithful and just to forgive us our sins, and to cleanse us from all unrighteousness. If we say that we have not sinned, we make him a liar, and his word is not in us." The passage here requiring confession that "*we* have sinned" is not limited to mean individual sin. It has a theological application. It refers to the sin which extends to the entire race, and has reference to the fall of man. John was orthodox on sin; that was the basis from which he started his full salvation appeals. Get men wrong on this idea of sin and you can never produce a healthy specimen of Christianity or have a gospel with the power of propagation. A man must stand four square on the subject of sin and the fall of man, or that man is a dead letter, so far as promoting the Gospel is concerned. His seeds are all sterile.

He may give them to the field, but they never sprout and bring forth fruit. The idea of the apostle was to get us down to bed rock on the subject of sin, both personal and racial. If we go back on that, we are not on common ground with him and are not able to go any further with the class of teachers which he represents; nor are we in line to partake of those depths of joy and peace and victory which he was so anxious should become the heritage of the disciples of Jesus Christ in all lands.

"If we say that we have not sinned" is parallel with the Apostle Paul's statement that all have sinned. All have missed the mark; the whole race has fallen short and will stay short until it is brought up by the redeeming grace of God. If we say that we have not sinned, which is the very central assumption of His word, then we go back on the entire program, and make Him a liar; we thus prove that His word has not found lodgment properly in our minds—"His word is not in us."

We wish you to look for a moment at the 4th verse, which seems to be the key to the epistle. There he explains why he writes this epistle. "These things write we unto you, that your joy may be full." This fulness of joy represents one way of apprehending the deeper life; otherwise known as the Spirit filled life; the consecrated life; the sanctified life; the higher life; or being established in grace. Here is a synonym for

EMPTIED AND FILLED 17

all of it. "These things write we unto you that your joy may be full." This joy is an exotic plant which does not grow spontaneously in the soil of this fallen world; which does not originate in the human heart; it is the joy of the Lord. We have a similar plant in the world, which we call joy; but it is superficial. It finds its root in circumstances; it depends on the weather, or upon our health, or how our friends treat us, or how enemies prevail against us, or our standing in society, or the condition of the crops, or declarations of war, or declarations of peace. There is nothing substantial or dependable in what the world calls joy; but God, through His regenerating grace, has given a peace, a consolation, which cannot be disturbed by changes in the weather, by the advancing of years, by reverses of circumstance, or afflictions of the flesh; a complacency that knows how to abound and how to suffer want; because this peace has its root, not in circumstances, but in God. An individual may not be able to shout when he has the chills and fever and rheumatism, but he may have this marvelous consolation as deep as the sea; far too deep to be disturbed by the ills of the flesh.

John assumes that his audience has a measure of this priceless joy, and he here announces his wish that they might have all that their capacity would admit; in the interest of their own efficiency, of course. This is a worthy object. Let a man prepare his message with this in view and he would seem entitled to a patient hearing, even if he were unskilled and awkward and given to offensive blunders. But when John the Beloved comes, announcing such a purpose with his message, we must sit at his feet feeling that of all the exponents of the gospel he has authority to speak upon this theme.

Ways and Means of Happiness

No matter where you find a human being, he is after joy. He may be in the brothel, or he may be at the seaside; he may be in the whirl of society; in the ball room; at the card table; or he may be in the church, the fashionable church or the unfashionable church; it matters not where you find a child of Adam's race, he is in quest of joy. But strange are the notions that people have of how it is to be procured. I suppose there is hardly a man or woman here who would not join me at once if they felt I knew how to get in touch with some great current of joy, and I should invite them to join me in an inquiry room that I might explain the secret to them. But it would be vain for us to invite you forward as direct seekers of joy. There is something underlying it and leading up to it which we at first must take into consideration.

Remembering the apostle's object, it is interesting to inquire into his method. We may safely regard him as an authority on his theme; but, supposing we have not examined his methods, and hearing his subject announced, should run out ahead of him and try to anticipate his formula as to how this joy may be induced. We might suppose that he would take us on an excursion among unfallen worlds; or show us the jasper walls and the gates of pearl and let us look upon the King in His beauty; with winsome words, he might tell us how the angels sing; and then, when we returned, we should be exceedingly glad. But that is not his method. There is one underlying principle in John's appeal. And I would say in passing, inasmuch as many of you are ministers and teachers of the Scriptures, we ought always to have our eyes on some definite and worthy object when we teach the Scriptures, and not be content with a general rambling in the fields of truth. John had an object, as he states; and he adopts a practical method for arriving at this object. The entire epistle drives at the thought that sin underlies our misery; that if we can discover the secret of getting rid of sin, we can discover the secret of joy; that in whatever degree we discover this secret of deliverance from sin, we have in that measure discovered this fulness of divine joy. The assumption is that if we cannot discover a complete remedy for sin, then this fulness of joy is impossible; but if we can discover a complete remedy for sin, then this fulnes of joy stands out among the beautiful possibilities that invite us onward in the Christian life. So really he gives us a treatise on sin and salvation; so clean cut and superlative that were it not inspired, we would regard it as extreme. There is not a chapter in which he does not make a strong deliverance on the subject of sin.

A Heavy Indictment

John begins his indictment of sin as the chief hindrance to Christian experience by asserting, "If we say that we have fellowship with God and walk in darkness, we lie"; we are not only strangers to the fulness of joy, but strangers to the initial installments; for no liar has any part with God. Darkness is a Bible type for sin. To walk in darkness means to live in the practice of some form of sin. Such a man is so far from fellowship with Christ, so far from the fulness, that he is not a partaker at all. The charge of being a liar is serious when it comes from Saint John. If some man with a low brow and a big jaw and a mean disposition should call me a liar, I should simply consider the source, and remember that hard words from a bad man may be a compliment; but when a man like John tells us that we lie, it is time for serious reflection. He teaches that if a man tramples upon the law of God, and then claims the knowledge of God, that man is a liar and the truth is not in him. Such a man preserves the delusion of antinomianism. Our Christianity must take a decided position on

EMPTIED AND FILLED 21

questions of right and wrong, and attach material importance to righteous living, or it cannot enjoy the initial consolations of the gospel, much less the fulness.

There is a principle involved in John's opening broadside against sin, "If we say we have fellowship with him and walk in darkness, we lie." One person cannot wrong another and still have fellowship. Your greatest enemy is the one who has done you the greatest wrong. Each sin against God puts the soul farther away from His fellowship. The coldness and enmity increases; the darkness deepens; till finally God is eclipsed; and the sinner, no longer realizing God's existence, vents his spleen against the Bible, the church, and the people of God. Hatred carries. If you hate a man, you lose friendship for his family, and will not build your new house after the pattern of his, or suffer the babes of your household to be given the same names that are worn by the members of his family. It is natural that we shall hate them that we wrong, and far from natural that we should have mutual interests and fellowship with one that we hate. It is therefore far from natural that any man who lives in wilful sin should have fellowship with God; and the apostle shows that instead of such people being headed toward the fulness they are headed away from it, toward the fulness of misery and woe.

But, reversing the operation of this principle,

John informs us that those who, forsaking all sin, choose light, and walk in it, shall have fellowship with God; and that such a life and such a fellowship will lead to a sublime consequence; the Christian will experience the *present, full,* cleansing power of the blood of Jesus Christ. In arriving thus quickly at this superlative deliverance from inward sin, John dashes off the first outline of his scheme by which he proposes to lead us into the fulness; that is, getting us emptied. With the emptying of the soul comes its filling; the one calls for the other and amounts to the other. The lesson is that men who would go up must first go down. If the Christians of Christendom, for whom this epistle is written, had known the full personal cleansing, they would have known the fulness of the blessing. And why did they not, and why do not some of us, know the full personal cleansing? Simply because we have not walked far enough in the light to see our need of it.

Deeper Experience Cannot Precede Intelligence

There is a principle in the laws of personal salvation that God cannot supply a need until we recognize it. He can only save us to a depth that we are able to confess and deplore. Only when we see the background of our heart, only when we see and deplore the subtle sinfulness of our inner nature, can the promise of cleansing be available for us; and only then can our fellowship with God be consummated, and only then can our consolation be full. Then, when we go to those who need a blessing, we shall be able to assure them from personal knowledge that there is a blessing for them. Then we shall no longer have to offer to the lost a gospel which as yet has not proved to be the power of God to our own salvation. Then there comes a deeper relationship with the Father, through Jesus Christ, by which a more intimate covenant of friendship is established. The soul of the believer enters into a significant league with God.

The Fulness that Fills

Every life is fraught with painful vacancies until it has its full quota of friendship and fellowship. No joy is full without friendship. Thus do we have fortune, thus do we have power; not in proportion to our silver and gold, not in proportion to the health and honor we enjoy. Our riches are measured by the number and character of our friends. I touch a vital question in your life when I ask you how many friends you have. As I hold up the fingers of my hand, let us count them. Name each one in your mind. Be careful to emphasize the word *friend;* reserve all the doubtful names for a more leisurely investigation, and name in your mind at this moment the list of those whom without hesitancy you count as your friends. Will the fingers on one hand be enough to count them? Let us look a little closer at these friends. Why are they your friends—why do they love you? Is it because of your physical attractions? Then, some day the wear of years and the ravage of sickness may rob you of that, and you will lose your friends. Is it because of your wealth? Tomorrow some frenzied world power may confiscate your wealth or storms may sweep it away and leave you a pauper; then your friends will be gone. Do they love you because of your influence, your high birth or political or social standing? Often the shifting sentiment of fickle society proclaims the first last and the last first. If ostracism should be your portion tomorrow you would at the same time lose all this class of friends. Is it your talent that gets you your friends? Are you an artist or a wise and gifted person, and, therefore, much loved and in great demand? Disease may begin with this evening's shadows, to invade your faculties and bring you down to the estate of a pitiful dependent. Then all whose friendship is based on this alone shall disappear out of your life.

If you will pay the price of this fellowship, if you will forego every prejudice and exalt the cleansing fountain which alike qualifies the high and the lowly for a divine fellowship, then I am permitted to present to you a Friend who loved you before you had any physical attractions, and who will love and cherish you as equally dear when the beauty of your youth has faded and your form is weatherbeaten. A Friend who loved you when no earthly goods were said to be yours, and who will love you when palaces have crumbled and gold has lost its value. A Friend who loved you when no one knew you, and who will love you as dearly when the world is pleased to have forgotten you entirely. A Friend who loved you when you had no gifts except to weep, and with whom you will be still in demand, still popular, when your right arm is palsied with age and your voice has lost its music; when men who send for you now and offer you employment shall forget you and turn to others; when in the solitude of old age or affliction you shall meditate alone in your quiet corner, forgotten in the scenes of active service, still this Friend shall cherish you, still He will need you. It will be His delight to uphold you.

"And when hoary hairs shall our temples adorn,
Like Lambs we shall still in his bosom be borne."

Such is the fellowship we find when in our heart of hearts we are willing to qualify for it, when we walk in the light, with no ambition contrary to that of realizing that the blood of Jesus Christ cleanseth us from all sin. Here is found a fellowship, a co-operation from the upper world, that makes life complete.

II

THE OBJECT OF POWER

BASED UPON ACTS 1:5, 8

"Ye shall be baptized with the Holy Ghost not many days hence." "Ye shall receive power, after that the Holy Ghost is come upon you: and ye shall be witnesses unto me both in Jerusalem, and in all Judea, and in Samaria, and unto the uttermost part of the earth."

THE words "baptized with the Holy Ghost" in connection with this passage seem to take care of an important distinction in dealing with the subject of the Holy Spirit. We are by no means shut up to the term baptism with the Holy Spirit in discussing these themes. The identical expression is not used in the forecast of the prophets to refer to this great divine blessing which was to come in the New Testament age, and it is not elaborately used by the apostles in referring to the fulfilment, in the epistles, which came later. But the fact that it should have been used at all, and, at one time, in the literature of the Gospel, used somewhat extensively, has its significance; because there is

THE OBJECT OF POWER

a distinctive meaning suggested in the words, "Baptize with the Holy Spirit." This distinctive meaning *may* be neglected in our articulation of the doctrine without any harm to the real results which we are due to secure in our own lives and under our ministry; but it may be neglected and the neglect lead to some teaching which would impair the force of our message and divert us from the deeper experience which God would have us to receive.

PERSONAL SALVATION COMPLETED

Evidently, the word baptize means to cleanse or purge. Such is its historic use. In such passages as John 3: 25, 26, it is used interchangeably with cleanse or purge. It is a noticeable fact that when our Lord is said to have received the Holy Spirit, which marked the beginning of His active ministry, the word baptize does not occur; for, while He properly submitted Himself to the ceremonial cleansing which is involved in water baptism, He did not need that cleansing which is involved in baptism with the Holy Spirit. The reason we would emphasize this baptismal attribute in the gift of the Holy Spirit is because, bringing in the idea of cleansing, it implies a greater conformity to the image of the Son of God. Referring to when it was fulfilled in him, the Apostle Paul tells us in Acts 15: 8, 9, that his heart and the hearts of his fellow disciples were purified by faith. Then a reference is made to the receiving of the Holy Spirit by the Gentiles, in Romans 15:16, where it is said that their "offering up" or their consecration was sanctified by the Holy Ghost. In the same epistle, Romans 6:4, 7, Paul refers to a baptism which accomplishes the destruction of the old man; the deliverance of the soul from inward sin. Salvation, or being saved, always refers to sin, in the Scriptures. It means to be saved from some form of sin, either actual or inward. We are told in Titus 3:5, 6 that according to His mercy God saved them by the washing of regeneration and the renewing of the Holy Ghost. This renewing of the Holy Ghost, which "he shed on them abundantly," was part of the process of their salvation. Thus, in this passage, he includes the gift of the Holy Spirit, following the regeneration of their hearts, as figuring in the completion of their salvation. The effect of the Holy Spirit being received by the disciples is discussed or referred to in such passages as Acts 4:32 and described as practically the same thing as that which was to be accomplished in answer to the Master's prayer for the sanctification of His disciples in John 17:17, 21.

So we mention this as an important distinction, because it would seem that, while some may have overlooked the distinction without falling into a hurtful error, others have fallen into hurtful errors by insisting that the fulness of the Spirit has nothing to do with completing salvation in the children of God. We mention the distinction because it is important that we should have in mind a desire to be more like the Master when we seek anything from Him; and, if we are, in a more complete sense, to be temples of the Holy Spirit, if we are to invite Him in to dwell and walk and live in us and minister through us, that which He is to find in us must be congenial with Him. Certainly we are not so by nature, and certainly we are not so until He fills us with Himself and consummates the work for which the blood of Jesus Christ is shed. The idea of the sanctification of a soul without the baptism of the Holy Spirit is as incongruous in the light of the Scriptures as the idea of day without sunlight. With day comes the light of the sun and with the light of the sun comes day; they are inseparable; the one depends upon the other. With the baptism of the Holy Spirit comes the sanctification of the soul and in sanctification of the soul comes the baptism of the Holy Spirit; thus, while the two terms sound and look decidedly different, they point to the same effect fundamentally in the experience of the believer. It is with these distinctions in mind that I call your attention to His promise of power. Power means ability to do; but before one can have that ability he must have some qualification of heart and disposition which makes him fit to be trusted with the power of the Holy Ghost.

Discovering Our Limitations

One of the most painful experiences that can come to a human soul is the experience of helplessness in the presence of some great task for which he alone is responsible. If not otherwise, some have had that painful sense of helplessness in dreams; as in the case of a nightmare, when we find ourselves in the presence of a swiftly moving train and unable to get out of the way, or a child is seen falling over a precipice or attacked by a mad dog and we unable to raise our voice of warning or lift a hand to help. In that condition we struggle with emotions that would choke us to death, were it not for the law of nature by which a man is awakened. But some of us take life so lightly and regard its duties and callings with so little seriousness that we never know what it means to have resting on our souls a responsibilty too great for us. If you have ever felt that helplessness, you were then ready to seek some promise by which you might get help and power and qualification for your task.

The situation is pitiful, when the devil comes into our homes and allures our child and drags him into the snares of sin and into disgrace and despair and death, and we are too weak to lift a hand of protest or engage in any kind of battle in behalf of that child. We discover our limitations when we go out to meet our obligations.

THE OBJECT OF POWER 31

We see the situation of a world staggering on in darkness, and we with our share of responsibility in coming to the rescue; yet we feel ourselves so weak that our weakness is utterly oppressive. Such feelings usually come as the experience of a soul awakened to duty. They more certainly come when he addresses himself to that duty. He may accept his calling from God and rise and go out in response to the great commission, before he discovers his helplessness. Usually when a man is called to a mission or some kind of rescue or salvage work to which his very best must be devoted, that man discovers his need of this promise which we have read you tonight, and is impelled to seek its fulfilment.

THE MAJESTY OF POWER

Power is one of the most majestic phenomena in all the realm of nature. Wherever we see a manifestation of power, we contemplate an attribute of God, who made the world. There is something magnificent in gravity, which holds the planets in their places and keeps them revolving around the sun. It is a silent force ordained in the universe, which no scientist has ever defined. That force has been here through all the ages. For many centuries in our own country there has gone down through the Niagara Falls a great volume of power due to the force of gravity; men have contemplated it only as one of nature's beautiful phenomena, without a thought of utilizing it; but finally they belted the wheels of their machinery to it and all such agencies, and the industrial world began to use the power of gravity. Today, great systems of railway traffic are conducted across the Rocky Mountains by the power of gravity. We are told that a man, experimenting with a potato on the spout of a kettle, contrived the notion that in the world there was some kind of force which, by the combination of water and fire, could be utilized; and so the industrial world hitched on to steam, and turned the old horse out to graze; and this mystic giant which had been stalking through the earth ever since Adam and Eve cooked their first breakfast in the garden of Eden, was hitched to our freight wagons and began to shake the continents with his power. It is a mysterious force as limitless as the millions of cubic miles of water in the sea and the billions of units of heat in the sun. Electricity has been in the crust of the earth and in all the elements above, since the dawn of the first morning. A man got a sample of it by sending up a kite. Then, after combining vitriol and zinc and copper and making batteries, they learned to make iron harness in which this great steed would work, and the industrial and scientific world began to turn the wheels of their machinery with his force. They made a messenger boy out of him and tied continents together, making neighbors out of the nations and whispering galleries out of the seas. Through all the ages it had been here, although there was not sufficient light and ingenuity to appropriate it until divine providence should ordain the time.

THE HIGHER FORCE

But there is a force more wonderful than this; a force quite as real, but it is of another character and refers to higher realms, more closely identified with the God that made the earth and created gravity and steam and electricity. Its existence is quite as literally true as electricity or any other force in the universe. It is the power of the Holy Ghost. For this there is no substitute; and we must learn by humiliating experience, if we cannot be taught otherwise, that the wheels of Zion cannot be made to turn by any power other than this. We may try the giant machinery of our organizations; we may try to use the force of education, literature, philosophy, and ingenuous appliances; these are all right in their places, but none of these can be accepted as a substitute for the power of the Holy Ghost. We must have this force, and until we have this, souls must be perishing whom we should reach, and we shall be unable to do the work to which the Master has called us. This is God's way, and we cannot find some other. This is the one force which is not derived by the skill of the inventor. They can not belt the wheels of their religious machinery to this by any kind of contrivance or ingenuity of this world. There is only one way into it, and that is to deplore sin and desire an uttermost deliverance from sin; a complete devotion to God who has called you into His work, with a view to the evangelization of the world. When we put ourselves in that attitude and commit ourselves to that program, we can get the power. It is through simple consecration and faith in God.

Some have gone so far, in less enlightened times, as to conjecture that the gift of the Holy Spirit is something peculiar to the apostolic age. They give their reasons for this, not in any direct statement of Scripture, but in the assumption that the Holy Spirit was given that men might work miracles. But miracle working power was not promised by the prophets in connection with this. Indeed the apostles worked miracles before they received the Holy Spirit, and many of them that received the Holy Spirit according to this promise never worked miracles afterward, so far as any record would indicate. We conclude that miracles have no essential connection with the baptism of the Holy Spirit. It is not given that men might do wonderful things, or attract the attention of the world by perpetrating some kind of sensation. It puts us on a plane of achievement where the magicians of Egypt cannot follow.

THE OBJECT OF POWER

IN TOUCH WITH FACTS

The object of this gift of the Spirit is not far to seek. A simple and direct reason is stated in the passage before us. It is that we may be witnesses unto Him at home and abroad, and unto the uttermost part of the earth. If this sort of program needs to be carried out, the promise of the gift of the Holy Spirit is as far from being obsolete at this time as it was on the day the apostles tarried in the upper room. If God needs effective witnesses today, and if the Gospel needs to be successfully published to all mankind, the promise of the baptism with the Holy Spirit holds as sure at this very moment as it did when Peter proclaimed his wonderful message to the people at Jerusalem, after he received the blessing in the upper room. At that time he told them that the great blessing which he had just received, the promise of the Father, was unto them and to their children and to them that were afar off, and to as many as the Lord should call. If He had said any less, our faith might have been unsatisfied; if He had said, "Unto you and your children," I might have thought I was not one of those children; if He had said, To those afar off, I might have said, I know I am a long way off on the map and on the calendar; but a good many other people are a long way off. If He had called my name, I should not have been certain it meant me, for some other men have that name. But He said, "Unto as many as the Lord our God shall call," and we who know He called us may know also that this promise is to us as much as it was to the Apostle Peter.

If the object is that we might be witnesses unto Him, the divine baptism must still be available; for He needs witnesses, more than He needs men in the ordained ministry; more than He needs young people's societies; or educational institutions. We grant He can use them all, but He must have witnesses. When He called the Apostle Paul, He coupled the idea of witnesses with the idea of the ministry; and the former is more universally indispensable than the latter. The work of world evangelism rests more on the office of witnesses, for which all God's children are asked to qualify, than it does upon the ordained ministry, to which only a fraction of the church is eligible. God may have all the pulpit preachers He needs, yet He cannot do this work according to His own plan unless He has witnesses. Witnesses are worth a great deal more than attorneys. Argument does not measure up with the direct evidence from a man who knows. The world is in need of men who know. The witness is not merely a man who thinks or believes; not a theorist, but a man who knows. Now that sounds high; it is rather strong talk; but the philosopher here knows the difference between faith and knowledge as used in a court

THE OBJECT OF POWER 37

of law and in the terminology of the Bible. He knows that faith is the acceptance of evidence; a perfectly rational thing, so much so that men do business upon faith. But knowledge grows out of acquaintance through experience rather than evidence. There is a realism in the statement and action of a man who was himself present when the thing happened, that can not be found in the testimony and ministry of a man who is sure that it is so but was not there when it took place. A witness is a man who was present when the thing took place. The judge says to the witness on the stand, "State what you know in this case;" and the witness says in answer to the judge's request, "My father and my wife and my pastor were down on the street, and the three saw the accused shoot the victim." But the judge says, "I have not asked you to state what they saw, I have asked you to state what you *know.*" And the witness says, "Do you mean to reflect upon my wife, and father and pastor, don't you suppose I know this is so?" Then the judge excuses him and says, "We do not ask you for what *they* know. We will call them for that." The court defines knowledge as what can be recited by one who was there when the thing happened. So in the Christian life, there is many a specimen of beautiful faith without experience; many an individual who has a doctrinal faith in God without a living knowledge of God or personal communion with

God. But he is not a witness. He may be an eloquent preacher; he may administer and preside over the organization of the church; he may be a writer upon Christian themes, thoroughly convincing in all his conclusions, but he is no witness; and God has to have witnesses in order to fulfil His plan for the evangelization of the world. These men who speak so fluently and beautifully must find a personal experience and get a knowledge of God, the deeper the better; the more full the better; not merely the witness of the Spirit, but the fulness of the Spirit. A witness is one who communicates evidence. He is not merely one who talks, but one who delivers the evidence and whose communication of evidence carries with it the force of conclusion. Many a man can get up in the witness stand and talk consistently and fluently, and when he goes down from the stand have had so many embarrassing antecedents that his testimony has no weight whatever in the case, but turns out to be an embarrassment to the individual in whose behalf he testifies. When a man knows God, he will talk, somewhere, somehow; he will get his mouth open under some circumstances; but the longest, strongest, most beautiful testimony that was ever delivered, to the saving power of our Lord Jesus Christ is a life of invariable Christian consistency, from the time one puts on Christ until the time he lays his armor down.

THE OBJECT OF POWER

Unanswerable Arguments

The words of the text suggest, in their order, the places where our testimony is to be felt. It is to begin in the home. "Ye shall be witnesses unto me at Jerusalem," means, to us, around home. Here we get closer to human nature than anywhere else; and human nature, no matter how sanctified it may be, has its frailties and weaknesses. The Apostle Paul advises in Ephesians IV that, to maintain the unity of the Spirit in the bonds of peace, they should forbear one another in love. Forbear means to put up with. He tells them how to do it, *in love.* We must not "grin and bear" the faults of others, but must *forbear,* in such a way that an individual who has faults and weaknesses will be no less free because of our presence and will not be embarrassed in our presence because of their faults. Jerusalem is an easy place to break down in your testimony and a fine place to seek an influence that will save souls and glorify God. If any one more than another is responsible for the salvation of your own household, it is yourself. There is no estimating the persistency with which the constantly wielded influence of a Spirit-filled soul will work conviction into the hearts of them next to it.

A son may go from a godly hearthstone, where Christ had a witness, into the cold skepticism of the world, and listen to arguments higher than his head; but when they have piled up objections too shrewd for his logic, he can point to the living witness at his own hearthstone and there is an unanswerable argument. I have found it true in communities where I have made evangelistic efforts, that if there were a few of these unanswerable arguments, it was not hard to have a revival; but if we were unable to find such witnesses, and were hampered by poor specimens, the results were poor. What we want most of all is unanswerable arguments, not in the pulpit, but in men who have salvation from head to foot and live it every day, letting their light shine with such compelling power that others, seeing, shall be constrained to turn to God.

The Undying Testimony.

Some one says, "I have lived that life, I have received that promise and by the grace of God, have been a witness unto Him; yet I have loved ones unsaved;" but if you are praying for your loved ones, and backing your prayers by a consistent life, enriched with the Spirit's presence, there is hope of their salvation. Do not despair, though you die without seeing the desire of your heart. I heard of a mother who lived this beautiful life and died, leaving an unsaved son who grew up to be a hard-hearted

THE OBJECT OF POWER 41

man of the world. After several years, while passing out of the hallway one day, he looked at his mother's portrait on the wall and some strange power gripped him. He found himself unable to move a step; and as he gazed at the lines of that saintly countenance his heart was subdued; and, kneeling down before his mother's picture, he gave his heart to God. He heard that voice more definitely than he heard it when she called him in childhood; he felt her hand upon his heart as consciously as he felt it upon his head when as a child he knelt beside her and said his, "Now I lay me down to sleep." Being dead she still had power; she was still presiding in triumph over that home where she had lived.

We have been in communities where such saints of God had lived and worshipped and had gone hence to be gathered to their fathers; already they were playing on their harps of gold around the throne; but they helped us hold our revival; they were at church; their lives were still being lived; their mighty spirits marched up and down those aisles and wielded an influence upon the hearts of the people which was incalculable; being dead they continued to speak. Such people live, right on, for years after their bodies go to the grave. When you go down to their grave on decoration day, every blade of grass thereon has a sermon for you. Every daisy that peeps up from the sod seems to praise the Lord, bringing the assurance to you that the blood of Christ can cleanse from sin, and proclaiming to the unsaved the reality of the religion of Christ. Some men, good men, clean in their moral habits and regular in their religion, can be very, very dead when they die. Oh that every one of us might have an ambition to live; not three score years and ten, but on, and on, in those communities where we serve. But let me caution you, there is only one way to do it; that is by securing in your soul the fulfilment of this promise in Acts 1:8.

Exalting Jesus

You may say, I wish all the ministry had it; I think it will help a man in his preaching. But it takes more grace to live it than to preach it. This is not a house plant, intended just to thrive in pulpits and theological libraries; it is for practical purposes; it enables you to honor God in the home; it is needed by the man in the shop, on the farm, in the law office. It renders religion successful in all the callings of life. It is not just grace to feel good and power to preach; it is power to meet the lion in the way; to resist the tempter in the trials of life and have victory, and keep our light shining, in spite of the world, the flesh and the devil. We cannot do it in our own strength,

THE OBJECT OF POWER 43

and some people say it cannot be done at all. *It can be done;* but there is only one way to do it, and that is by the power of the Holy Ghost.

It is a very good thing for the ministry, as proved, for instance, in the life of Apollos (Acts 18: 24-28). A devout man, eloquent, and mighty, in the Scriptures; but there was a depth of experience in the grace of God, to which he had not gone. The presumption is strong that it was the same power of the Spirit of which we speak; for Luke, who wrote the Acts, is about to recite the incident of the twelve disciples receiving the Holy Ghost under Paul in that same city, when he tells us that Aquila and Priscilla, Paul's old associates, hearing Apollo, discerned that he needed to go deeper; and, taking him to their home, taught him the way of the Lord more perfectly. It is a sign of grace, I may say in passing, for a minister of Apollos' parts to sit at the feet of a plain layman and woman and be taught the deep things of God. Becoming as a little child to get into the kingdom, he had continued as a little child, to stay in. The effect of his deepening is plainly seen, when we compare the results of his service at Ephesus, before, with that of his service at Corinth afterward; in the meeting at Ephesus, nothing is said of the audience being drawn to Jesus; they were impressed with Apollos. We can imagine them as they went away from the service, saying, "What a great preacher he is"; but in the service at Corinth, though he preached with the same eloquence, they lost sight of him and saw Jesus. The longer he preached, the more beautiful Jesus became; they saw Jesus at Pilate's judgment seat; they saw Him ascending Calvary; they saw Him rising in clouds of glory, they saw Jesus at God's right hand; and the old Jews said to each other, "I believe our brethren have made a great mistake; I never felt so clearly or saw so plainly as today; we have killed the Messiah, I am convinced. I will confess Him, if they turn me out of the synagogue." Thus he mightily convinced the Jews, and that by the Scriptures, that Jesus was the Christ. So at Corinth he had power to show them Jesus; and when his meeting there had ended, we might have heard the people saying, "What a great Saviour we have!" It is said, "If I be lifted up I will draw all men unto me;" and how can He better be lifted up than in the lives and testimonies of His disciples; how else indeed may He be lifted up? It is plain that the promise we find in the text of this evening represents God's way of qualifying us as representatives of Jesus Christ.

I trust that you will open your heart in prayer. I shall in due time call on you for an expression; but I cherish some kind of hope that if you have not yet received the promise, you will come into the experience before you are

THE OBJECT OF POWER

called upon by me. It does not require a great ceremony in order to get this promise fulfilled in your soul; all you need is to commit yourself and accept the promise, letting Him have His way in your life. It is entirely possible for you to get this while you sit in your seat at this moment if you open your heart, and abandon yourself to Christ. Oh how much hangs on this! We cannot afford to be superficial or diffident in this matter. We are here to do business for eternity. We are summoned to be at our best for the great work to which God has called us.

III

THE FAREWELL SOLICITUDE OF JESUS

BASED ON JOHN XVII

"Sanctify them through thy truth."

OUR Lord was about to finish His ministry in the world. It was the night before the crucifixion. Hitherto He had been associated with His disciples. At most, they had been separated from Him but for a little while and would return to receive inspiration from His presence. Now they were to have this privilege no more; and along with the loss of this privilege were to come added responsibilities. Their horizon was to be enlarged; their field was to be widened; their trials were to be even greater; and, while previously the world had learned some ideas of God through beholding His Son, who was God manifest in the flesh, hereafter they were to get their ideas of God from His disciples; and all the spoken messages which were to come, hereafter, were to come from the lips of His disciples.

All this rested upon the mind of the Master

FAREWELL SOLICITUDE OF JESUS

when He prayed the prayer recorded in the 17th chapter of John, called His high-priestly prayer. So He specialized in that prayer, with this in view. His words portray the emotions of His great heart; and it is interesting, in the midst of such contemplations, to go through this prayer and note the direct petitions that it contains, and then the reflections which He makes upon those direct petitions. All this seems to be thought out and breathed forth in the prayer.

Having read the passage, we shall notice some of its salient features, before entering upon our main outline of thought.

A Double Preservation

In the 15th verse, He prays for them to be preserved, in a double sense: "I pray not that Thou shouldest take them out of the world, but that Thou shouldest keep them from the evil." That is His unique way of praying that they might not die; that they might not be killed or come to an untimely end without having finished the commission which He had given to them severally; and that carries to you and me its like meaning. As much as to say, I pray that thou shouldest not take them out of the world; that no accident might suddenly deprive them of their lives; that they might be kept from all evil, temporal and moral. The meaning applies to both forms of evil. So it is a prayer that they might be kept from shipwrecks and tragedies and fatal diseases; in other words, that they might be immortal until their work was done. You have heard the expression, "Man is immortal till his work is done;" but that is subject to qualification. You are immortal till your work is done, provided you put yourself on God's altar and go about your business, proceeding to do your work; provided, moreover, that you pray and live to that end. Only under those conditions can I have that kind of faith. But we do have the prayer of Jesus back of us in this instance as a shield against any accident or event that might overtake us, provided we are in the path of duty. It is wonderful what life assurances, what splendid accident policies, a man can have, when he is living in the divine order and his heart is kept in unison with the will of God.

Not of the World

"I have given them Thy word; and the world hath hated them, because they are not of the world, even as I am not of the world." Bear that last remark in mind, because it seemed to linger with Him as one of the sweet consolations. Twice in the prayer He says they are not of the world. Evidently this means that one's citizenship is in Heaven; and it also means that they were above the vile and doubtful things in which this world indulges. If you or I, as pastors, had a church with a membership of which we could say this without any exception, we should feel that we had a great church. You will bear in mind that this is the kind of people He is praying for. You very well understand the New Testament meaning of "the world." In the ninth verse we learn that He is not praying for "the world." This is a strange expression, but will not be so strange if you take the right view of the prayer; for though He prays not for the world, the world is on His heart (v. 21); and He prays admitting that if His prayer for the disciples is answered, the world's chance of salvation will be much better.

Through the Truth

It is through the Truth that this prayer is to be answered; there must be the attitude of the convinced judgment as well as the surrendered heart before the heavenly Father can find it possible to fulfil in us what is intended in the prayer. If there are reservations and doubts and well-founded prejudices, even such as may be entirely consistent with a devout heart, it would be difficult, it would be impossible, for the Father to do this work. You will note that it is purely a divine work, due to be accomplished when the individual is ready. Jesus asks that

God shall do it and that He shall do it through the Truth. I would recommend that we always seek the truth and make ourselves the slaves of truth, without attempting to state our preferences as to what the truth should be. Being the slaves of truth is the only way that we can keep from being slaves of fear, or of sin, or of circumstances, or of unhappy emotions, or even of unfortunate dispositions. By becoming the slaves of truth, we can be made free from everything else; for "whom the truth makes free is free indeed." So Jesus identifies the truth here with the releasing cause of the soul's sanctification. When I was able to put myself in line with this and it became clear and consistent and unmistakable to my judgment, already leaning God-ward as hard as I knew how, but very careful what I committed myself to, when I had no longer a mental reservation, but was satisfied in the depths of my soul that it was undoubtedly the truth, the question of consecration was incidental. That was already settled. The question of taking God's way was not to be discussed: that had already been discussed and concluded. I simply arose to my feet in my room alone and said, "It is the truth;" I seemed to rise in a new atmosphere and my head seemed to touch some kind of cloud that brought divine glory into my soul. Somebody says it is by faith; that faith is the releasing cause; which, of course, is Scriptural;

but faith, though present, is so axiomatic as a mental state that you can hardly sense it, when the truth gets absolute possession of you. Faith defies all analysis; it is such a simple fact of consciousness that you can scarcely examine it in a psychological way at all. Faith is just taking it. When the truth takes you and you take what the truth stands for, you take it without effort. You do not wait until someone asks you to go through a certain system of prayers and groanings. It might be well to do that and to go through whole nights of it, as Jacob did, if that is the way of getting your poor old stubborn self in line; but if we can find a way of making our hearts and minds conformable unto the truth, and dismiss from our minds every opposition to the will of God, if there remains no longer a question, and we fully follow the Lord, the matter resolves itself into a very simple transaction in which we do not need the help of priest or preacher; in which we do not need our friends to gather around and lay their hands on our heads; but in less time than it takes to recite the terms, we can rise and be conscious from head to foot that we have met God in a way that we have never met Him before.

For the Winners and the Won

"Neither pray I for these alone, but for them also which shall believe on me through their

Word." I have two interests in that verse. One is because of the fact that it includes me in the Master's prayer. The other is because it clearly indicates God's plan for the evangelization of the world; that God purposes to do it through human instrumentality. If the saving truth is conveyed to the lost nations of the world, it must be conveyed, not by the voice of angels, nor by the thunderings of the elements, nor through any of the agencies of nature; it must be delivered through human lips and illustrated by human examples. The Master intended that these should be the convincing forces; that the hearts and lives and tempers of His disciples should illustrate God's nature and God's laws unto the children of men everywhere, and that their testimony should bear fruit in the faith of other peoples who would be added to His kingdom.

Knowledge is Experience

"That the world may know" (v. 23). This is a step higher; a stronger apprehension than that in the 21st verse, where He prayed "that the world may believe." Belief is a stepping stone to knowledge. It was not enough for men to be intellectually convinced and added to the program, to increase the membership and swell the numbers of the Church of Christ. A faith that does not lead to an experience is not fulfilling

FAREWELL SOLICITUDE OF JESUS 53

what it was intended to accomplish. We noticed on last evening that experience was a synonym for knowledge; that when the judge said to the witness on the stand, "State what you know in this case," he as much as said to the witness, "Give us your experience; tell us, in brief, what you saw or heard or felt." Jesus wanted the world to have in His disciples a convincing agency, but He did not desire that their conquest of the mind of the masses should be all. They were not to be satisfied with the bare achievements of adding adherents to the creeds of Christianity; He wanted them added to the experiences of the New Testament. They have to believe before they can know.

THE WORLD'S GREATEST LESSON

Upon this 23rd verse I may add, He wanted the world to find out by experience that He loved them, through contact with the disciples. Oh, you say, is this poor old, heart-broken, darkened world shut up to this one way of knowing that God loves it? Can't it find that out from the beautiful flowers that grow? Can it not learn that from the azure skies and the twinkling stars? Do not the birds proclaim it in their songs? Does not all nature herald that great doctrine of the love of God? It does not. It is very eloquent in proclaiming many of the attributes of God, but that one attribute, calculated to break the human heart and turn man to

God's saving grace—the love of God—that one attribute is to be brought to the world through you and me; and if we have not enough grace and blessing in our own souls to let the world find it out, they will die without the information. If you are going forth as the herald of the cross, convincing the world that God is good, that He is great, that He is powerful, that He has a law, that He has a judgment, that He has a Church, unless there is in you that grace and blessing and personal experience by which they shall be convinced also of this one truth, God loves me, you are not doing your part. And that is the reason Jesus prayed this prayer for them; it was because He knew that they needed this experience, whatever it is; and you will note, I am not talking dogmatically as to what it is. The only thing that I insist that you shall agree with me upon at present is *that* it is, not *what* it is; I want your company as far as possible down the road, and I feel that I have your approval, so far, in stating *that* it is. We shall inquire what it is later. It seems from this and the ensuing verses of the chapter, that if anything were ever clearly to be inferred from any passage, it is clear that He is praying for His disciples to be made perfect in love in order that they might be successful conductors of the one great thought on which the salvation of the world depends and that is that God loves the world.

FAREWELL SOLICITUDE OF JESUS

Now in a little more orderly way, I shall invite you to some expressions in this lesson. We shall link them together; they are separated in their rhetoric, but they are closely identified in their sense. The expressions which we shall link together, you will find in the 17th, 21st and 24th verses; and if you care to do so, you may underscore these expressions and indicate the connection between them.

"*Sanctify them . . . that they all may be one . . . that the world may believe . . . that they may behold my glory.*" We are going to reverse our order in reflecting upon these thoughts, and begin with the last contingency.

"BEHOLD MY GLORY"

The time was when we looked upon that expression as perhaps designed to decorate the passages of the Bible, with no very essential meaning; but in studying kindred expressions through the Scriptures, we discovered a definite meaning underlying the thought of beholding the glory of God. Moses prayed, "I beseech thee, show me thy glory." The answer to the prayer came in this way; God took him into a hiding place in the cleft of the rock, covered him with His hand, and passed by, permitting Moses to see Him. He could not stand to see much of God, but he was permitted to see all of God that it was possible for him to endure, under his present condition.

When Jesus was talking with the sisters of Lazarus, whose faith seemed to be hesitating at the grave where their deceased brother was interred, He reminded them of a former conversation, saying, "Said I not unto thee, that, if thou wouldst believe, thou shouldst see the glory of God?" Then their faith rallied and took hold of the promise, and Jesus raised their brother from the dead. They saw the hand of God made bare; they saw a manifestation of divine power which could not possibly have been duplicated by any of the occult forces of the world; which could not have been imitated by any rival that the Lord might have.

In wanting us to behold His glory, evidently He desires that there should take place under our labors and ministry and in our places of worship, manifestations of the divine presence upon such a scale and in such a form that they cannot be attributed to hypnotic or preternatural forces, or any of Satan's varied ways of imitating the power of God. Such imitations are illustrated in the power of the magicians of Egypt. The work of Jannes and Jambres is being perpetuated today. That is, when we do a thing, the enemy gets himself up a bunch of heretics to refute in some way the works of God by working some similar thing through them.

No doubt that we have had some healings in that grotesque institution which we have over in Utah, called Mormonism; there is no doubt

FAREWELL SOLICITUDE OF JESUS 57

that the movement under Mrs. Eddy in America has produced some cases of physical healing. It may be confined to a certain class of physical maladies, and we have no doubt that many of the so-called cures of "Christian Science" are of troubles that were only imaginary at the outset. But occasionally they do something which men of medical science and men of the religious world are unable to explain. Satan did that in the time of the magicians of Egypt; and you may count on this, that if there is any circumstance by which he can release the power of disease, and, by so doing, capture a man's gratitude, destroy his belief in saving truths, and get his clutches on a human soul, he will do it.

There may be things in our religious meetings which, though not of Satan, are not of God. These may be called wonderful, by short sighted people who cannot see to the botton of the thing; but God is anxious that we be so closely connected with Him that it will be possible for Him to bring about things under our ministry which Satan cannot duplicate, which the rivals of the Gospel cannot produce, and the supernatural character of which is undeniable. They never broke the power of the devil upon a man; they never pulled poor old Jerry McAuley out of the gutter and made a saint out of him, to rise as a tower of strength and bless his fellow creatures in the world. There are some miracles that the teachers of false doctrine and the repudiators of the atoning grace of Jesus Christ can never work. They can produce phenomena that are at least preternatural, and we are too limited sometimes in our power of analysis to tell the differene between the preternatural and the supernatural; but God is able to do things that every man must acknowledge is a manifestation of God's power; and when once you meet with such a manifestation of God, you will never be quite the same person again. It will make such an impression upon you that you could go for days on the strength of it; you could go for months on the strength of it; you could go for years on it; indeed, I think you could go three score years and ten on the strength of it.

"Is not faith sufficient?" you ask. Should I ask to walk by sight? Is not the promise, "Where two or three are gathered together in my name there am I in the midst" sufficient? That is all true, and we delight in it; but when God in His great mercy sees fit to manifest Himself in some way that we are bound to recognize as His presence, when we feel a strange hush come over our spirit, and that heaven and earth have come in touch with each other, then that which seemed afar off begins to seem near. The great facts of revelation assume the proportions of reality. The prayer of Christ provides, not for just one divine event in life, but that we should have, as often as needful, manifestations of God's glory. If the church of Christ will let the prayer of Jesus be answered, and be more increasingly weaned from the world, setting her heart on the will of God, He will put her in a place where He can manifest Himself on a larger scale than ever in the history of the Church; and I cherish the confidence that the Church of Christ is going to do this, in her best representatives. It appears that even now we are facing a great divine event, and I look toward that event with unspeakable joy. We are going to see the glory of God. We are seeing the horrors of hell. Hell has been belching forth in all its fury for the past three years, doing its worst. We believe if God can find a people through whom He can work in His Church upon earth, He is going to answer this movement from hell by a great movement from heaven, and that we are going to behold the glory of God in a way that will balance these horrors of hell which some of us hardly dreamed were possible five years ago; but He will have to get us in shape before He can do it, and this is His way to get us in shape. He has but one way, and that is to let the answer to this prayer take place in our hearts.

For a World-wide Revival

"That the world may believe" is one of the objects of His prayer. We remember He said, "I pray not for the world, but for them which thou hast given me." That sounds paradoxical;

for it seems He was praying for the world, but it was indirectly. He meant that His direct prayer was for the Church, and He saw that if He could succeed in praying an effective prayer for His Church, He could do more than if He were going out in a direct appeal for the unsaved multitudes. It is in view of this essential law that our representatives call together a convention for the deepening of spiritual life. When we become burdened and pray effectively for the sanctification of the Church, He will accomplish much toward the salvation of the world. If we can get the Church to put on its beautiful garment, to arise and adorn itself in the glory of God, we shall do more for the world than we could through any eloquent message put forth on the desert air. The expression "That the world may believe," seems to involve this: that if the Church gets sanctified through the truth, the conversion of sinners on a vast scale will become entirely possible and quite probable. But I also read another thought which is seriously implied there; that is, if we, as the people of God, do not let the Lord's prayer be answered in our hearts, the probability of the world's blessing drops decidedly. It then turns out that it is not very reasonable to expect the world to believe on a large scale, unless we induce this cause which the Master deems the logical cause. If this is God's way of producing widespread results in the conversion of souls, it

FAREWELL SOLICITUDE OF JESUS 61

would be fanatical for us to expect these results without seeking the answer to the prayer of Jesus in our own behalf.

SINGLENESS OF HEART

When our Lord prayed, "Sanctify them . . . that they all may be one," He realized that, if the prayer were answered, there would be produced in all of His disciples, of all persuasions and nationalities, a singleness of heart, a unity of sentiment, and an agreement as to their points of emphasis, which would aid in the evangelization of the world. Oh, you say, we are doing that by the federation of the churches; we are doing that in Karuizawa, when we meet in our committees. We get closer and closer together, we learn to sympathize with each other and love each other better. All that is very good and important, but that will not accomplish the object. You may thus *approach* the object, but not *arrive* at it. We can only arrive at it in one way. The Master has laid down that way; that is, to let Him have His prayer answered in us, regardless of our denomination or nationality. When He says "that they all may be one," certainly He does not mean to pray that the Frenchman might become an Irishman or the Englishman might become a Spaniard. He does not mean to pray that the Presbyterian might become a Baptist or the Baptist a Methodist, or that you might lose your denominational distinctions and individuality of convictions in the incidental interpretations of the Gospel. He is praying for a higher unity than that. He is praying that they might be one in heart. People may be one in doctrine and two in heart, or they may be two in doctrine and one in heart. Give me the latter every time if I desire a great force against the kingdom of Satan. The fact of a man's denomination is a very trifling matter so far as it affects his usefulness and standing before God. I do not mean that it does not matter what a man believes. That position in itself is heresy; it may lead him to a great disloyalty to Christ, and violation of the law of God; but the matter of his denomination is a small thing. I have known people to say that it was a great sin in Christendom that so many denominations existed. I do not undertake to say that every denomination is providential or divinely organized, but I do not doubt that the various Christian denominations in the world and the different religious organizations have been permitted of God, and, in a way, approved, as suiting the conditions of the age in which we labor, meeting the demands of our temperaments, and providing for our infirmities. I think it quite a fortunate thing that everybody does not belong to my church. That may not be your way of looking at it and therefore I do not charge you anything for the suggestion. I am not crying out against the existence of the various denominations as though they constituted some great sin in the sight of God. But the grace mentioned in this prayer will bring about a unity of heart and revise our scale of emphasis. Anyone who gets this prayer answered in his heart is likely to get the bottom knocked out of some things which he cherished. It is characteristic of a man with not very much grace to holloa loudest on the things in his creed which not very many people believe, and talk the softest on the great fundamentals, upon which the salvation of the world depends; but when a man gets a sufficiency of grace, he begins to emphasize the fundamentals upon which the salvation of the world depends.

In our country we have great plains which are made into plantations. They do not all belong to one farmer; but when you go through after the crop has grown, you may think they all belong to one field. The cross fences are there; but when the crops are prosperous, you lose sight of the cross fences, and seem to see only one farm. The effect of the answer to this prayer in the hearts of the believers is no longer to see cross fences as the main thing about the farm. You will begin to see that the main thing about the farm is the crop.

THE FAR REACHING REMEDY

What does the word sanctify mean? You have agreed with me already that it means something; thus far we have gone together charmingly. I think, since we have examined the effects which it was designed to produce in the hearts of the believers, you will agree with me that it must mean a great deal. We have all heard quite a babble of definitions for that term, but I think those of you who are more familiar with its original root will agree that it is one of the most powerful words in one of the most powerful languages; and you will find a lexicon of good standing which will bear me out in the statement that the word sanctify means all it can. This fact is sustained in the passages of Holy Scripture where the word is used. I am trying to say this: Its meaning is only limited by the object to which you apply it. You apply it to a garment and it means, the garment must be physically clean, and devoted to sacred purposes. It cannot mean more, because the garment has no greater capacity. It cannot mean less, because it always means all it can. You apply it to Christ Himself, and we understand it means that He consecrated Himself to the great work of communicating holiness to the unholy by His sacrifice on Calvary. It cannot mean moral cleansing, for He needs no moral cleansing; but it means all it can. Apply it to man, and it means that man must be wholly devoted to God; that his talent and his time must be consecrated upon God's altar and his moral nature must be cleansed; that he must

FAREWELL SOLICITUDE OF JESUS

have God's Spirit. It cannot mean any less than that because it can mean that, and it never means any less than it can. Numbers of people can be found among the Bible characters, and many whom we have known in the Christian Church, whose testimonies command our respect, who say that with them it means all that is here stipulated.

He was praying that this might come to His disciples. How do we know that they needed it? Oh, you say, "They all needed the new birth, but it was not possible for them to be born again until Pentecost; it was impossible for them to have a spiritual experience or a change of heart before." I suppose you would grant that if it had been possible, they would have had it. They would have had a supernatural experience before Pentecost, inasmuch as they were the first chosen disciples, getting instruction from the first year of the Master's ministry. But let me affirm that it was possible. If Nicodemus would have responded fully when he came to Jesus, it would have been possible for him to be born again. This doctrine of the new birth was presented to him not only as possible but necessary. We remember another character who was not very highly favored nor very much respected; that was the woman at the well. He told her that if she had asked, He would have given her living water, which would be in her, a well of water, springing up into everlasting life.

It was possible during the ministry of the Son of God to have very much of a New Testament experience. We call your attention to the fact that there are in general two dispensations, the old and the new, and that these overlap each other in the ministry of Christ, for about three years. His ministry represents a distinctive dispensation which was transitional in its character. It partook of the nature of the old and of the new. In the beginning of His ministry the old dispensation began to pass away and the new dispensation began to come in. Then, the old came to its conclusion and the new dispensation reached the full height of its meaning with the coming of the pentecostal Spirit on the souls of the believers after the close of our Lord's personal ministry, to which we may refer as the dispensation of the Son. It is a little short-sighted to make the statement that the disciples had no sort of a Christian experience before the day of pentecost; for the Master had said, "Now ye are clean through the Word which I have spoken unto you," and had told them to rejoice that their names were written in heaven. He was praying for those whose spiritual status was exactly what the spiritual status of every one was due to be when he became a Gospel believer; for He prayed not for them only (verse 20), but for all future

FAREWELL SOLICITUDE OF JESUS 67

believers. Thus is it clear that He put the spiritual attainment of those immediate disciples for whose sanctification He prayed, on the same level as those who were to become believers after pentecost. Whatever may be said of pre-pentecostal believers, when He prays for post-pentecostal believers, He indicates that a man is justified before he is sanctified. No one holds that there was to be a dispensational limitation in the experiences of believers after pentecost.

You say, I never heard of a real Christian who was not sanctified. We do not wish to draw our audience out in an exercise of spinning fine theories, but we are told in the 5th Chapter of Ephesians that Christ so loved the Church that He gave Himself for it that He might sanctify it with the washing of water by the Word. That looks as if a real Christianity, minus sanctification, might be possible. There was such a thing as a Scriptural Church, unsanctified. A Church that Christ loved, and in which He was greatly interested. There is still such a Church. Giving Himself, He made a wonderful investment, to accomplish that thing in His Church; and certainly He is going to cling to His Church and urge its attainment of this grace, seeing He has invested so much in it. Oh, that His Church might prepare to see His glory; that it might respond to this wonderful investment, and become a glorious Church, not having spot or wrinkle or any such thing!

IV

PURSUIT AND POSSESSION

BASED ON I CORINTHIANS XII AND XIII

"But covet earnestly the best gifts: and yet show I unto you a more excellent way."—1 Cor. 12:31.

THE Epistle to the Corinthians in its signature is addressed to the Church at Corinth. "To them that are sanctified in Christ Jesus, called to be saints;" that is, to them that are provisionally sanctified in Christ, and called to be sanctified in themselves; and, further, he goes on to address it to all that in every place call upon our Lord. In the flow of his discussion throughout the Epistle, he refers to various classes of people at Corinth. Not that he addresses the letter to all; he discusses some classes who were holding membership in the Corinthian Church, who did not deserve to hold church membership. At the juncture of our lesson, he takes the question of advancement in the Christian life. The 12th chapter is a discussion of spiritual gifts; a discussion of those things which equip one to become better known in the activities of the Church militant; to be more conspicuous on this present stage of action. But when he finishes this discussion, he turns to another, which to his audience was very important; for they, being Greeks, sought perfection in gifts. He turns to a discussion of grace; more grace; a discussion of the vitals of religion; of more religion; another sort of advancement, that does not pertain to one's spectacular talent. He treats this as something which, though it may not make the individual any more conspicuous in this present world, will make him better known in the world to come; and which, even should it fail to make him more interesting to the church and to his fellow men, will make him more interesting to God and the angels, and provide him with a greatness which will be recognized in the world to come.

These other things are not to be under-estimated in their place. The gifts will afford a man the facilities to become useful in this present world. But, as he very clearly indicates in the latter verses of the 12th chapter, the gifts are not universally available. They have often been very extensively withdrawn, and I do not doubt that some of them have been entirely withdrawn from the Church. True, these signs were to follow them that believed; but they were not at all times to follow all that believed. They are not the indispensables; but he proposes, having discussed them, to turn the attention of his audience to one indispensable element of progress; and, conceding that they should "covet earnestly the best gifts," he proposes to show them something better than gifts; a more excellent way. This is another way of saying, a more excellent Christian experience, a deeper work of grace, a definite enlargement in the vitals of the Christian religion.

A Sure Evidence of Life

There is something in the heart of one who is converted to Christ which always aspires upward. It is characteristic of them that have risen with Christ that they are seekers; they seek those things which are above. The analogy of the child of God and a human or natural child carries quite strikingly at this point. There is a psychological quality called persistency in the child, which orders his progress. He is always pressing onward and upward. He is headed somewhere in the direction of progress. This explains a child's propensity to play or raise a disturbance. If you could totally prohibit this in a child, there is no calculating what would happen to him; he would explode, or die. Obedient to that strange law called persistency, the child is impelled onward. The best authorities on dealing with children tell us that we should have fewer dont's and more do's in our code for the child. If you want him to quit this, give him another job; he has got to have a job. There is little use for you to say when you find him tugging at the lace curtains, "Quit it," unless you give him something else to do.

The Lord's children are that way; they are going on. If there is no seer to outline for them the terms upon which they may make progress according to the Scriptural order, they are going to make some kind of progress; they are going sideways, if not straight; they must go wrong if they do not go right, but they are going. It would seem that the many tangents and fanatical movements in the Christian world are quite natural and logical. If among the natural leaders of Israel no voice has sounded out in clear notes, instructing the children of God upon holiness and the deeper life, showing them the true road of progress, it is no wonder that many have turned to the fanatic by the roadside who claimed to know how they could get something farther on and better. It may have been anything but good for them; but they had that persistency which had to find its answer. In the absence of the right answer, they found the wrong answer. With the child of God, it is onward or die; and, sometimes, when error prescribes the path of progress, it is onward *and* die.

Be Saved from Ambiguous Terms

How fortunate it is if we, as so many of us professionally occupy the place of leaders, can get a clear vision upon the advanced truths of the Gospel and be able to take care of that matter for those who are in our flock. The Apostle Paul is very careful there. He was no less definite in dealing with the deeper truths, no less faithful to his flock, than in the initial truths of the Gospel. Sometimes we find it very easy to be definite and even radical on the elementary truths of the Gospel, but when we get into the deeper truths, we begin to talk Greek or something else our audience cannot understand. Often it is because we ourselves have not got a clear vision of the truth. Once I was riding a pony from Alexandria to Marksville, La., when I was a boy preacher. After I had got a little way, I came to the home of a Frenchman who knew a few words of English and asked him to direct me to Marksville. He proceeded to say, "You go down this road till you get to the corner, and then you turn," and then he began to indulge in a volley of Acadian French. He was quite definite in starting me but when it came to the further instructions, to the more remote part, his instructions ceased to be intelligible. We, as Christian leaders, should be able to talk in the vernacular from first to last. The Apostle Paul, who gives us this wonderful lesson, talked in the vernacular all the way through into the fulness of the blessing of the Gospel of Christ. I may further emphasize the fact that before we can give the directions, we must have acted upon the directions ourselves.

When we seek for the deeper things of God, we are not merely taking care of ourselves, but carrying out the theory of the apostle to the Gentiles, who said to the elders of the Church at Ephesus, "Take heed unto yourselves and unto the flock." A man who does not take Scriptural heed to his own religious experience is not fully qualified to take heed unto the flock. This is our apology for holding conventions for the deepening of the spiritual life of those who stand out as leaders and workers in the vanguard of the Lord. No man need be ashamed or embarrassed to be found in an inquiry room or at an altar of prayer seeking something deeper and greater for his own soul because of the fact that he has a position of prominence in his Church. It is an honor and a credit to him to be taking care of his own spiritual condition, because that is the only logical way for him to look to the better spiritual condition of those who are under his care. Indeed the New Testament soul winners did not enter the harvest till they had full salvation. They tarried.

What Paul Showed Them

The Apostle proceeds at once to show them the more excellent experience. He does not use a label in this instance, but simply describes the thing. He does not say, I will name a more excellent experience for you, but I *show* it to you; and it is evident that the 13th chapter of 1st Corinthians represents his effort to carry out what he proposes to do. The tense and tone of the passage indicates that he is pointing out a life upon which they might immediately begin to enter, by faith. He outlines it in a word picture, so that anyone may be able to see the experience to which he is inviting them. He holds it up before them in such a way as to invite them to seek it. The object of presenting this to the disciples at Corinth was that they might become interested in it and anxious for it. It is a very fortunate thing if we are able so to present the deeper experiences of the Gospel that they will become interesting to the people whom we wish to help; so attractive that the people will be induced to thirst, and to say, "Give me, Oh give me, that life." Paul draws a most successful picture of the more excellent life. He personifies it, giving it hands and feet and lips, and tells us how it behaves itself. Before he does that, he emphasizes its greatness and magnitude, by contrasts. He says it is greater than eloquence, greater than knowledge, or prophecy or sacrifice. Telling us what it will do, he says it does not behave itself unseemly, it suffereth long and is kind, it beareth all things, believeth all things, hopeth all things, endureth all things. And when he is through with this personification, he begins to tell us of its lasting qualities. Some of the most durable things in the world have their day and fade away; but this something which he is presenting to us will abide to all eternity. John Fletcher, I think, is author of the suggestion that these beautiful New Testament pictures of a higher Christian life are not given for the purpose of teasing the Lord's disciples. They are not given for the purpose of interesting us in an impossibility. They are certainly calculated to produce in our hearts aspirations, if we are living as consistent children of God; but they are not intended to produce empty aspirations. They represent something which answers to the aspirations of the Christian heart. It will not do to say that all these pictures of possible Christian experience represent essentially the experience which everyone must have in order to deserve the name of a child of God.

Take the Mean Between the Extremes

We have two classes of extremists. One is the class who say that these standards held up in the Scriptures are unfeasible and never intended to be realized by the Christian in this life, and the other class are those who say they are the only standard by which a man can be recognized as a Christian at all. The latter class of extremists are cruel in that they would exclude many whom God does not exclude. Sometimes men produce the latter theory for the sake of some prejudice which they hold against the subsequent work of grace, and only adhere to it when convenient. It would be incorrect for me to say that any man not measuring up to the 13th of 1 Corinthians was not a Christian, but was a child of hell. On the other hand, it would be an evidence of a dull spiritual leader if I should say that this man cannot come to a better experience than he has. We sometimes meet with people who have taken a fancy to a low standard of Christian living, who seem to think that it fosters the spirit of humility for them to hold and profess a low standard. I have seen a few who actually argued against the feasibility of Bible standards, going so far as to pronounce the ten commandments too high for us. They said the ten commandments were God's straight edge which He intended us to stand up by to see how crooked we were; but that we could never be that straight. So, some have assumed that such standards of Christian experience as we have found portrayed in the passage which we have read this evening are God's agencies to stimulate in us higher aims, but that

PURSUIT AND POSSESSION 77

we are not expected to attain. We are not so apt to fall, they say, when we are aiming high. Thus they advocate everlasting pursuit without any possibility of possession.

A Legislator of one of our states comes into the legislature and says, "Gentlemen of the Legislature, I wish to present a bill for the enactment of a law in this commonwealth. The following is the proposed law. You will recognize at once that the law is all but superhuman in its demands, and you will understand, when I explain that I do not expect the people to carry out those demands or live up to this law. I intend, Gentlemen of the Legislature, that this law shall stimulate our citizens by keeping them everlastingly aspiring to a higher standard of citizenship, even though they should always fail to live up to it." We do not doubt they would put such a man out of the legislature. Men sometimes take this view of the law of God, and too often apply the same principle to the standards of the New Testament, assuming them to be unfeasible, holding that God does not mean we should come up to the standards, but that they are simply there for the purpose of stimulating within us a desire for higher things so that by our everlasting pursuit, even though possession is impossible, our characters shall become stronger. If the Lord should lay upon us demands which are unfeasible, it would be unreasonable. Every demand that God makes implies a promise of grace to enable us to meet that demand. He never told a man to do a thing that the man, by God's grace, could not do. We conclude that Paul's outline of the higher Christian experience as given in our lesson, is equivalent to a promise that God will give us that very thing, and that it represents his effort to stimulate us in its pursuit. If you were to convince men that this were unfeasible, then the pursuit which some people say is so healthy and happy would be unreasonable. We could not get a man everlastingly to pursue a thing which it was impossible for him to find. If this pursuit contributes anything to a man's character, there must be some hope of possession. Otherwise, when he acquires information enough to see that his pursuit is vain, he will give up his quest and surrender, and lose that element in his character which was induced by the exercise of pursuit.

Prevents the Shipwreck of Sound Ideals

A certain young man came running to Jesus and gave evidence that for a long time he had been seeking for the secret of eternal life. He finally found the terms upon which this perfection of grace might be had, counted the cost, and, deciding that the price was too high, turned away sorrowfully. All through the past this pursuit and this hope had sustained him and

PURSUIT AND POSSESSION 79

served to make him into a beautiful character, one whom the Master admired; but the incentive which had sustained him to that moment was cast down, when the conditions were considered, the terms rejected, and the pursuit abandoned. Not much could be expected after that in the moral and religious life of the man; for, giving up his pursuit, he instantly lost the incentive which had sustained him.

It is a fine thing for you to seek holiness, even supposing that you would be so impractical in your views that you spent a long time seeking without finding. There is something in the exercise of seeking that causes one to be a better man; not only a better man, but a happier man. Any man, from the day that he makes up his mind to be all that God wants him to be and find all God has for him, is a safer and happier man. If there is a Christian here to-night who would say in his heart, "From this time forth, by the grace of God, I shall seek for this deeper experience; I sign up from this moment in the sight of God to be a seeker at His mercy seat till I find His fulness," that man would find himself girded from that moment with new strength. The object which he had set his heart upon would inspire him; though his Pentecost be long deferred, if that man held consistently to his purpose, he would rise as a tower of strength; there would come a new light of joy in his soul. After the ascension, when the disciples had purposed to tarry in Jerusalem till the full blessing came, they returned from Olivet with great joy, and were continually in the temple, praising and blessing God (Luke 24:52, 53).

It is a great thing to make up the mind to be all that the Lord wants us to be. It would be a high day in your life if you would bid farewell to any sort of compromise, and make a covenant with your heart that you should have nothing less than God's best. When you get this far along it will be a high day for the work you serve, even though ere you return, you may not be able to say, "I am sure that when I come unto you, I shall come in the fulness of the blessing of the gospel of Christ." But this is a fulness which, I am glad to tell you, does not have to be deferred.

Possession Sublimer than Pursuit

We have had many a High School debate on the question, "Wherein is the greater joy, in pursuit or possession?" Sometimes one side wins, sometimes the other. Indeed on many questions by which this problem may be illustrated some minds may be in doubt; as, for instance, a question of politics or matrimony. But my mind has long since been settled in regard to this subject of perfect love, that while the pursuit is very interesting and inspiring, and while it has in it elements of joy from the very

PURSUIT AND POSSESSION

moment the heart sets itself upon the theme, pursuit by no means equals possession. "The heaven of heavens is love." It is the active principle of Scriptural holiness; and nothing else that men may ask you to seek, aside from this, is worthy to be compared with it.

I went down the street of a certain city and came to a beautiful building with a glass front. The whole front was a show window. It was high noon and I had not had much breakfast. Just inside that plate glass on a nicely covered table was a roast turkey, a broiled fish, a fine dish of sauce, a beautiful loaf of bread, and several other things which would sound good if I should describe them. Do you know why they were there? They were there for the purpose of stirring up in me the appetite that I had, in order that I might come in and pay the price and get my dinner. That is very simple; but do you suppose there was any door? I never saw a situation like that where there was not a door somewhere for me to get in; but it was not all door. You do not even have to make the door conspicuous. You can count on a man who has the hunger and the price, to find the door. He may make two or three mistakes; he may get into a shoe shop or an elevator shaft, but you can count on him, if he is hungry, to recover himself and back up and come again until he finds the door that leads to the place where these good things are to be secured. Talk about theories of the fulness of the blessing; it is not the theory but the experience which we desire. It would be a great mistake if we should exalt the theory above the experience. The theory is the door. There is some theory. Everything has to have a theory, even the making of cake or pie or the doing of mission work. There is some theory that will get results; and if you have been tampering with a theory that did not get results, just back up and get a theory that does. We should not for a moment set our heart upon any sort of theory merely for the sake of that theory, or because some one else held it, or because we had already said something and did not want to go back on what we had said. It is not hard for a wise man to go back on a thing if he has made a mistake. I have found that though the fool does not change his mind, the wise man does. A hungry man may dive in at the wrong door, but he will not stay long in a dry goods store or an alley because of a conceit that refuses to retrace its steps.

What would you think of a man who walked up to the show window and looked in and after he looked at the good things for a moment, made a face at them, showed signs of nausea, and turned up his nose and walked to the other side of the street? I would say that he was sick; and, instead of needing a restaurant, he needed a drug store or a doctor. That is true with us spiritually, if when there is presented to us these feasts for the soul, our souls seem to say within us, I have no interest in such things; I am afraid we are sick, and need a healing touch. We should become alarmed about ourselves if we are not interested in the blessings which God holds out for us in His Word.

A Word to Timid Souls

I do not know whether all of you would be interested in a bit of illustrative talk which you may regard a little light for this occasion; but I heard of a gentleman who went to dine with his friend. They had a sumptuous meal, and he noticed an old Newfoundland dog, resting at the door of the dining room, with one corner of one eye open. Every time a child would drop a crumb, that dog would get up as deliberately as a bishop and walk down to the chair and pick up the crumb with all the formalities of a ceremony; and, smacking his mouth on it with a great deal of relish, would turn and march back to the same place in the corner, lie down again, and shut his eyes, keeping a sly watch on the table. He said he noticed the dog's seeming appreciation for small things, and when he was through with the meal, he gathered a pile of nice fragments, sufficient to fill one plate heaping full, and took the plate and set it down right by the old dog's nose. Then the dog raised up and looked at him and looked at the plate of food in a kind of inquisitive way as if to say, "It is too good to be true," and deliberately turned around and walked out of the house.

Permit me to exhort you tonight to examine yourselves; and if you find no response in your hearts to the promises of God for a deeper life, for a sanctified life, for a victorious life, for the very best life that can be found in the New Testament, go and see if you are not suffering from some spiritual ailment; and get the divine touch upon your soul. You may have come to feel that though these testimonies sound good, and though this experience looks exceedingly desirable, it is too much for any poor mortal in this life to expect. The thing that led you to that attitude may seem to be a commendable virtue of humility; but it is in fact due to some habit of thought from which you should be delivered. God wants you and me at our best. He wants us at our best not merely for our own sake, but for the sake of His great name, for the sake of His Church and of a lost world.

V

SEE YOURSELF FIRST

BASED ON ISAIAH VI

"Woe is me! for I am undone."

THIS vision of Isaiah has its sequel in the missionary spirit which seems to have taken hold of the man (8th verse) as a result of the experience through which he had just passed in the vision. There is, no doubt, much unrecorded history connected with this appointment which Isaiah was about to accept, and which he probably had the opportunity to accept many times before, but was not so disposed, because he did not have the spiritual qualifications which he needed to incline him toward it. The missionary spirit has many definitions. It may be the motive growing out of our humanitarian disposition to help uplift our fellow beings; it may be the impulse, born of the statesmanship which we possess, to bring the world up to a state of civilization; or it may be that wonderful instinct of the heart which is changed by the grace of God. In this latter meaning the missionary spirit is an exotic plant which never springs up in any soul unless it is planted by the heavenly Father's hand. A man who has that form of the missionary spirit will serve on hard scrabble district more complacently than any other type of missionary, and will be reconciled, when he knows that God has sent him to his post, whether he sees the chips fly as he could wish, or not.

Heart Language the Same in Every Age

The experiences of the saints of the Old Testament differ somewhat from the experiences of the saints of the New; and yet we learn that through tremendous strides of consecration and aggressions of faith, some towering characters among the patriarchs of old partook of experiences strikingly like those experiences of grace which were to be proclaimed as universally available in the New Testament era. Due to difference in dispensation, there may be some technical differences in the experiences received by such men as Isaiah and David and Jacob in the Old Testament, but they strikingly illustrate the divine work which is provided for all of our souls under the Gospel dispensation; and it is with a view to this illustration that we wish to apply the experience of the Prophet Isaiah to our own religious lives this morning.

SEE YOURSELF FIRST 87

THE CONTAGIOUS PROPERTIES OF GRACE

God's plan, as you have observed scores of times, and as your presence in your field of activity proves, God's plan for the salvation of the world is to use human instruments. His children, as we see plainly taught in Matthew 13:38, are the seed of the Kingdom; and I have the conviction that there has scarcely been a man converted in the supernatural New Testament sense, who had not at some previous time in his life, been touched by some child of God who had a positive experience of grace in his own heart. You may say that you have seen hypocritical men, who were strangers to anything like a work of grace, preaching, even holding great evangelistic meetings, and causing people to become converted; and that among the number of their professed converts you were sure you saw some who were genuine. But if you will trace the history of those converted you will usually find that their lives had been touched at some former time by a person of vital Christian experience. From this we gather the importance of having not merely a profession or an orthodox creed, but a sound and positive experience of the grace of God in our own hearts, before we go ourselves to execute that glorious commission which we have the honor of receiving.

I will carry that a little further and say, it

does not now appear, in the average case, that a man can come into this deeper life of the soul which we are trying to study in these services without having at some time come in contact with an individual who had received the pentecost in his own soul. It is not enough for him to have clear teaching in the matter; but he must, figuratively speaking, have laid upon him the hands of those who have received their pentecost. By having their hands laid upon him, we do not mean in any formal way, but we mean to say that the usual divine economy for multiplying this great movement is to have God's people come in contact with some one who has an experience in his own soul to match that experience which God wishes to impart to them. There are circumstances where this would be very hard to accomplish, and the circumstances would, I am sure, seem to make an exception to this rule. There are people who have come into the experience of full salvation without chart or compass, without human leader, or teacher, or theory; for the simple reason that the main thing about it is not a shibboleth or a point in theology or a matter of theory. Yet the *rule* is for God to send someone to us to whom He has introduced this glorious secret in order that they might impart to us the secret. You see an illustration of this frequently in the New Testament. I have in mind especially the instance in the Acts of the Apostles where Philip had held a remarkable revival in Samaria and many were converted. Shortly afterward two men who were acquainted with the deeper things of the Gospel, namely, Peter and John, came down and presented the fuller truth to these converts whose lives, through the preaching of Philip, had been so marvelously revolutionized. These ripe ministers led them into a deeper experience, which they referred to as receiving the Holy Ghost.

A Pioneer In Bible Holiness

But Isaiah lived in a day when there was no man to send to him in order that he might get a deeper experience in his soul. He was a young prophet at the time of this testimony which he gives; he was to become a conspicuous figure in the history of true religion. He was destined to be called the Messianic prophet, and to be honored with more realistic visions of Christ than any prophet of the Old Testament. He says this marvelous experience came to him in his young manhood as a prophet; in the year that King Uzziah died. It was during the administration of Uzziah that Isaiah began his ministry, and he was to be a prophet through the reigns of Jotham, Ahaz and Hezekiah. God had no man to send to this young man to help him into a deeper experience. In order that he might fill the great place God had laid out for him, it was necessary that he should have a definite advancement in his religious life; and I may whisper to you that the same is true of a large number of you, if I may say it modestly, and I am sure I am willing to include myself in any sort of confession at this point. God has a great work for all of us. It may not have the magnitude of the work of Isaiah; but before God can ever expand us to where we shall be large enough to fill the place that He has for us in the fields He has mapped out for the ministry of our lives, He is going to have to give us a deeper work of grace.

Deep Answereth unto Deep

No man has had a consistent and powerful solicitude for the salvation of the lost among whom he labored until he first came to an ordeal in his own religious life which led to a crushing solicitude for his personal salvation; until then he is incapable of it. He can have a statesman-like solicitude, or a humanitarian solicitude; but not a prophetic solicitude for the salvation of the people among whom he labors, unless God can give him light enough and conviction enough to crush him down at some time in his religious biography over his own personal salvation. God wanted to get Isaiah into the deeper experience presented in this Scripture, and it appears that He had no man to send to him. In the case of

Hezekiah, who also received a marvelous deepening, and got to the place where he served the Lord with a perfect heart, we can see that his experience was brought to him through Isaiah, who was his pastor; but what is to be done with Isaiah, in order that he may have the experience God wants him to have, so that he can fill the place God has mapped out for him in the great program? There seems to be nothing left but to take him into a vision and in that vision let down a section of divine worship in its ideal form and let him go to that service attended by ideal worshippers, where there was ideal music and ideal singing, where the order was just as the order ought to be, where God held the place He ought to hold, and where the atmosphere was just what it ought to be. So, under some strange circumstances that we are not in a position to explain, Isaiah had a vision. While it was a vision, everything connected with it was not fiction by any means; more especially is the latter part of it fact. The transaction turns from fiction into fact before the vision ends. A fact takes place in his heart; a fact takes place in his attitude toward God's call and commission; a fact takes place that explains his wonderful life, the tremendous victory of his soul, and the immeasurable usefulness with which he is credited.

When the Seer Saw Himself

Let us go with Isaiah for a little while and attend that service; let us notice the impressions which he obtained and the manner in which he received them. The first impression that comes to him is the place that God occupies in the service. He saw the Lord high and lifted up. In that circumstance of ideal worship God was greater than the creed, greater than the architecture, greater than the order of worship. He was greater than the music, or any of the ministering agencies. He saw the Lord "high and lifted up," occupying His proper place.

Then he saw God's followers there. "His train filled the temple." The character of those who were there were "God's train," those who followed Him consistently, consecutively; they were all there and they filled the temple. He was impressed with the fulness of the audience and character of the attendants.

Then he saw conspicuously the seraphim, who seem to be symbolical of those agencies in the church which apply the Gospel and administer the saving grace of God. The evangelistic and missionary agencies which characterize the ideal communion of worshippers.

Then came the song. He remembered a strain of its refrain and recites it as he tells the story of his experience. The refrain seems to be a kind of index to the subject matter of the song rendered by that heavenly choir. It ran like this: "Holy, holy, holy, is the Lord of hosts; the whole earth is full of His glory."

In connection with the song, he was impressed with some kind of agitation which conveyed itself to him through the moving of the posts of the door. Something, I presume, like that which we have felt in the midst of a spiritual service where one of the brethren, tremendously concerned about the salvation of the lost, was described as nearly "praying the roof off the house." The posts of the door were moved at the voice of him that spoke. Any church that is normal, any church that measures up to the heavenly ideal in its solicitude and concern for the salvation of the lost will be marked by agitations of some kind. Sam Jones once said, "Where there is no agitation, there is stagnation."

Isaiah was impressed next with the atmosphere. He said, "The house was filled with smoke;" the fragrant incense which accompanied the worship. When we speak of a spiritual atmosphere in our worship, it is more than a figure of speech, as some of you who are spiritually discerning can confirm. There are places where you can read and understand God's word, and where you can speak it with greater freedom. Nor is this all due to psychological conditions; much is due to the atmosphere, in which Satan and evil influences may gain or lose their liberty. This often determines the extent to which the grace of God and the Word of God may have free course. It is observed in the latter part of Joel's second chapter that under pentecostal conditions an atmosphere is created, so that it becomes easy for a man to get converted. It shall come to pass that whosoever calls upon the name of the Lord shall be saved. In some places it is easy to get people saved, in other places it is hard, due to that unanalyzable something which we call spiritual atmosphere.

The next subject of attention with Isaiah was himself. You might suppose that a man of sincerity and devotion like this young prophet would be delighted with such a service, and exultant all the way through; but it was not so in this case. A healthful atmosphere does not make some people feel good. If a man has lived in a land of malaria, down in the swamps, having been born and reared there, and knowing nothing else, he may carry much malaria and not know it; and if you ask him if he is well, he will say, "Quite well"; he means comparatively well or as well as any of his neighbors. So far as such people are able to imagine what it means to feel well, they think they are feeling well. But take a man of that kind and bring him into the mountains, where the atmosphere is anti-malarial, and he will feel like going to bed; he may have a spell of fever and have to send for the doctor and take a dose of calomel. Not that there is anything wrong with the atmosphere, but there is something wrong with the man, although he did not know that there was something wrong with him, as he compared himself with his neighbors. The Apostle Paul brings out this thought in Corinthians when he says, "They, measuring themselves by themselves, and comparing themselves among themselves, are not wise."

Responding to a Conviction

And so Isaiah got into this atmosphere; and though he evidently felt himself in a pretty good condition with reference to his relationship with God and his call to be a prophet, he became very sick in his soul. But we give him credit for accounting for it with marvelous astuteness. I am charmed with the candor with which he met the facts when brought face to face with the facts. I heard of a man who acted differently. He came to a meeting where the atmosphere was similar to that which Isaiah described, a tabernacle meeting which I know was all right. He was a good man, a Christian minister. He had heard unusual reports about this meeting, so he attended, to investigate. He sat in a convenient place, feeling that he could trust his judgment, as he knew he was a Christian and his heart would respond to anything that was intelligently spiritual. He had been in many services where heart searching was not very deep and the atmosphere not very fervent and he had had a high time religiously and called it a revival; but when he got to his place, the truth began to search his heart; the atmosphere was glorious, and other people were enjoying it; but this man became very sick in his soul, and seemed to say, "There is something the matter with me or there is something the matter with this meeting. There is nothing the matter with me; therefore, there must be something the matter with this meeting, and I am going to leave it"; and he left it. But Isaiah comes up under similar circumstances, and takes the other branch of the conclusion. He says, "There is something the matter with me, or there is something the matter with this service. There is nothing the matter with this service; therefore, there is something the matter with me. Woe is me; I am undone"; and in a most striking way, by the grace of God, he began to discover his trouble. What was the matter with him? He puts it in figurative terms, saying, "I am a man of unclean lips." I do not think this means that he used tobacco. It does not seem that a man of Isaiah's rating in the service of God would use tobacco. Nor did it mean that he told unclean stories. Indeed, you are not to take him literally. It seems evident that he was a man of magnificent ideals, and that he thought he was all right; but that this meeting sprung upon him a tremendous surprise. Any man who is a student of manifestations of the mind is bound to see that the prophet Isaiah entered into a surprise and awoke to a brand new situation. The sequel of the lesson, and what he received after his collapse, proves to us that by the figurative expression, "a man of unclean lips," he means that he discovered, away down in the innermost recesses of his soul some dross that needed the fire of God to burn it out, something contrary to the nature of God; and that that discovery overwhelmed him.

Isaiah's New Theology

He awakens to the fact not only that inward depravity, "sin in believers," is experimentally true, but also that it is theologically true. "All of my crowd is in the same condition; I dwell in the midst of a people of unclean lips." Theological discoveries are often the concomitants of experimental discoveries. When God has a chance to deal with a man's soul on these deeper lines, it frequently necessitates a revised theology. Many sincere men, who purpose to be logical, have their theological system somewhat revised through entering into this experience of full cleansing. When men run across some practical discovery, when they drop their pick into some gold mine which they had overlooked in the great provisions of the gospel, there must come a theological development to correspond. Thus promptly, before he left the mourner's bench, when Isaiah made this discovery about himself, he made also a discovery with regard to human nature in general. Just as in his own soul he needed the refining fire, the refining fire was needed also for others. Happy is the man who goes exploring in the wonderful mysteries of the gospel of grace, and, making discoveries for himself, makes discoveries for others also; and happy is the man who has the candor and frankness to own it on the spot and act upon the conviction which God has given him.

When Earthquakes Form Continents

Isaiah was not a man content to have in his heart something that ought not to be. We fear this is not always the case with Christian people. Some of us are sometimes quite complacent when we know that there is something in our heart that ought not to be there, and that we have settled down on a plane of consecration and service that is beneath what we know God wants. If this be the case with you, you will stay right there, at best; and, at worst, you may drop to a lower plane than you intended. The man who is complacent to find in his heart dross that ought not to be there, and in his consecration defects that ought not to remain, and in his devotion imperfections that are utterly unneces-

SEE YOURSELF FIRST

sary, the man who will then go on and eat his dinner and sleep soundly, and sing his songs and preach his sermons, will never get anywhere in the way of spiritual progress, to put it mildly. There is a certain cataclysm of soul or paroxysm of desire which must precede our full salvation. Dr. Talmage once said, "It takes sanctified recklessness to win souls." We may also say, it takes a kind of sanctified recklessness for you to get into that definite experience of grace which is held out to believers, in the word of God. In the various Bible characters this is illustrated over and over; and I am sorry for those who are so gradualistic in their philosophy and so essentially wedded to all of the tenets of evolution that they cannot see that just as there have been cataclysms in the history of the world's present formations there must be cataclysms in the history of the formation of a great soul in the service of God.

Man's Extremity

Now if you are satisfied, you are as far as you are going to get in spiritual advancement. If you see definitely an experience of grace for you here, and say, "While I would like very well to have it, I see how I can get along without it," you will be very sure to get along without it. The only man who ever gets this cleansing fire in his soul as experienced by

Isaiah, and others, is the man who comes to a juncture in his life where he cannot get along without it; who affirms that he cannot and will not get along without it. Jacob at Peniel said, in substance, I will die or have the blessing. I am here to stay until I get it. I will not leave this place unless thou bless me. Isaiah said in substance, I am a ruined man; I am going no farther; I am undone. He was not only undone but he was done. That is the extreme feeling that often comes upon a soul that gets in great earnest to find the blessing of the fulness of the gospel. And a soul that is too nice and too aesthetic to permit himself to fall into this extremity of desire, and force the issues against his evil self, delivering his carnal nature up for crucifixion, is too nice and too aesthetic to have the fulness of the blessing of the Gospel of Christ. You have got to be undone. Man's extremity is God's opportunity, and you must get to where your self-sufficiency is gone. The word undone in this passage is the opposite of self-sufficiency. Any man who cherishes in his conceits one vestige of self-sufficiency may as well make arrangements to get along without his pentecost. When this man reached his extremity, God's opportunity came. One of the Seraphim took a coal of fire with the tongs, from all the altar, and laid it to his lips and said, "Lo, this hath touched my lips; and thine iniquity is taken away, and thy sin is purged."

We must not understand by this symbol that the prophet received a mere local application; he received a constitutional treatment, that struck at the seat of the trouble. "Thy sin is purged"; not that some of the branches were knocked off of a tree of bad habits, but the great deep of his inner nature was cleansed. Iniquity means unevenness. It is the up and down life. We have in some places what we call corduroy roads; where rough logs are laid across boggy places; it is pretty rough riding but it prevents you from sticking in the mud. A Christian life may be very genuine, and yet it may amply illustrate the words of the old negroes who used to sing, "Jordan am a hard road to travel, I believe." The unevenness is taken out of our spiritual life when our sin is purged.

The Candle of the Lord

But why did they tell him that? Do you understand that a man needs the Spirit to bear testimony to this deeper work? There is evident proof in the Scriptures that the Spirit will bear testimony to the work of God's grace and to all of its stages in the heart. "Why," you say, "if God does such a work in the heart, does it not shine in its own light, and why is not that sufficient?" You have forgotten the greatness of the soul. The human soul is one of the greatest beings in the universe. It is deep and intricate and wonderful. It is as deep as the heavens. The study of the human soul would be as great as the study of the astronomic universe, in whose vastness men discover new constellations as they are able to enlarge their telescopes with which to see. As in the bosom of the universe, we find intricate laws and new mysteries, so in the human soul, made in the image of God. So great is this mysterious soul of ours, so intricate its laws, so unapproachable are its mysteries, that we do not know what is in us unless God tells us. You can never say, I have gone through all the ramifications of my nature and I know there is nothing of this in me. Only as God takes His search light and goes through you, do you know what is in you. David did not think he could take a stroll through the avenues of his soul's mysteries and say, "There is nothing in my heart that ought not to be there." He seemed to feel that the human soul was so intricate and so unsearchable that he could not fathom it, and so he prays to the God who made it, "Search me and know my heart and see if there be any wicked way in me." No man shall ever know all the things in his soul that ought not to be there, nor may he ever know that all is taken out of him, excepting as God tells him by the convicting illumination or the comforting testimony of the Spirit. One may know that certain evil is in him because it asserts itself, and he recognizes its ugly visage; but it may be so subtle that he may not know. My heart may deceive me; therefore, the only assurance that my heart is conformed to the will of God and clean through and through by the blood of Christ is the testimony of God in my own soul; and if I will put myself in the place where God can have His way with me, and be sure that there is nothing I want quite so much as His perfect will done in me, it will not take very long for Him to reach me with His baptism of fire which takes away the dross, and then to whisper in my heart this wonderful information which He is always so glad to impart, as He whispered it to one of old, who, before his translation, had "this testimony, that he pleased God."

VI

THE GREAT TRANSACTION

BASED ON ROMANS 11:33–12:2

"And be ye transformed."

WE would designate our study this evening, as St. Paul's altar call to the brethren. We shall give special attention to Romans 12:1, 2. Paul was a constructive theologian, and one of his masterpieces is the Epistle to the Romans. Those of you who are familiar with the contents of this wonderful piece of literature will perhaps recognize in each instance the relationship of title to contents as I give a key word to suggest the theme of his several chapters in succession. The first chapter we should call Depravity; the second, Impartiality; the third, Lawlessness; the fourth, Justification; the fifth, Grace; the sixth, Deliverance; the seventh, Sin; the eighth, Assurance; the ninth, Sovereignty; the tenth, Righteousness; the eleventh, Mercy; the twelfth, Perfection; the thirteenth, Subjection; the fourteenth, Prudence; the fifteenth, Gentile Hope; the sixteenth, Cooperation.

THE GREAT TRANSACTION 105

To Be and to Do

In the twelfth chapter, we come to the summit of his great discussion. The foundation of the twelfth chapter is in the first two verses. The balance of the chapter, you will remember, is a beautiful code of practical ethics, one of the most attractive deliverances on Christian decorum that is to be found anywhere. It covers all our relations, including our relation to the brethren, our relation to the church, to the business world, to strangers, to friends, and to our enemies. In short, it tells us how to *do* as Christians; but the New Testament never fails to recognize the fact that before a man can do he must be. More than that, the New Testament so clearly assumes the fact of our depravity and of our native delinquency that it teaches before a man can be, he must become. These two first verses of his practical chapter on the Christian life tell us not only how to be but how to become.

A Standard Consciously Chosen

He begins his appeal to the brethren by saying, "I beseech you." That seems to safeguard their free moral agency; that is, he assumes to say, I am going to place before you a new standard of consecration and devotion which it is your privilege to meet, which you do not have to meet, but which I beg you to accept. It is a fact that every step we make in our relation with God involves somewhat of choice on our part. You did not become a Christian by accident. There are none of you quite so loyal to the five points of Calvinism that you believe you became a Christian without your will being involved in the transaction. It never occurred to you that God arrested you by some irresistible force and, without your consent, dragged you into His service. All of you are pleased to acknowledge that you gave yourselves as volunteers in the army of the Lord. But this truth carries also into the features of the deeper Christian experience. When there come to you definite stages of progress in the divine life, they are going to require choice and purpose. It would occur to you from the words of the Master when He said, "The Kingdom of heaven suffereth violence, and the violent take it by storm," that for a man to become a Christian, he must not only be willing, but tremendously determined; and just as that is true in the initial requirements of the Christian life with which you are all familiar, it is true with the advances in grace which are represented by the promises and pictures we have read and discussed in our lessons from day to day. You will never accidentally stumble into the grace which is represented in the passage I have chosen for a text this evening. You will never go to sleep with a defective consecration and wake up with a

THE GREAT TRANSACTION 107

full consecration the next morning. There is no chance of your mixing and mingling with the people that have all the joy and fulness and peace that comes with complete consecration and thus absorbing the same yourself. When you definitely come to this experience, it will be because of your deliberate purpose and choice. It will amount to a transaction, and you will be absolutely conscious of the transaction and of your own determination. This does not mean that you can *will* yourself into anything. This does not mean that you can pull yourself up to a work of grace. God has to do the pulling, but He has to have your consent and not just your passive consent. He will have that too, but first it requires your active consent.

Sufferers and Saints

"I beseech you, brethren, by the mercies of God." God's mercy is one of the strongest attributes on which to base an appeal of this kind, because if there is anything calculated to stir a man to the deepest devotion to the Lord, it is an acquaintance with His mercy. I have been impressed with His attributes of power, of greatness, of justice. I may have gained such impressions from the heaving waters of the ocean, from the majestic heavens, and from the beautiful sceneries of nature; but I never felt so greatly moved by these things to devotion and to a deeper consecration as when I came in contact with an exhibit of His mercy. When I see a great exhibition of His mercy, I always want to bow down and worship before Him and offer Him a better offering than I ever did before. You will notice that the people who have had more trials and more occasions to test the mercy of God average up to a higher standard of consecration than the others. I do not know why it should be, and yet it is a fact of history, that those who mark the highest standard of devotion are those who, in the providence of life, have had occasion to experience greater degrees of God's mercy, so that the greatest sufferers have often been the greatest saints. It is not because their suffering has made saints out of them, though the fact that great sufferers have been great saints has led some less discerning Christian writers to suppose that there was some essential connection between suffering and saintliness. There is no essential cause which explains saintliness excepting the blood of Jesus Christ; but it has been demonstrated that when a man knows a great deal about the mercy of God, you have something on which to base an appeal for a higher standard of consecration.

Our Own Spirit Bears Witness

"I beseech you, therefore, brethren, by the mercies of God, that ye present your bodies;"

THE GREAT TRANSACTION 109

that is, your whole being. The body, being the tenement of the soul, is mentioned for the whole man. We present the soul along with the body and as we cleanse the body, God cleanses the soul. We take hold of ourselves by way of matter (v. 1); God takes hold of us by way of mind or spirit (v. 2). The word "present" means to turn everything over and take your hands off and call it His. Now that is a transaction which is purely your own. You have the power to do this as a believer in Christ, in one definite event; and when you have done it, you will know it without any supplemental witness. You will know it by the testimony of your own consciousness, just the same as if you had turned a piece of property over to your friend. You did not have to have any witness to that, excepting the testimony of your own consciousness; and with that there went also a consciousness that the friend assumed the responsibility of taking care of that property. Your part of the deal came to an end the day you turned it over to him and said, This is yours; I give it to you. There was a kind of rest that came to you naturally. Such a rest is felt as a natural consequence by every man who learns this great secret of turning himself over as a living sacrifice in consecration to God. It is a kind of crossing of the Rubicon. You know that you have turned it over and are content that the transaction is done. You feel relieved; your struggles have come to an end; your name is signed to the contract. Some people may take that for all there is in a higher Christian experience beyond conversion; but that is only a psychological experience; and, though it be very blessed, it is transitional; it furnishes us the ground to trust God for a supernatural work. You have the right to expect that upon this sacrifice there shall come, as came upon the type of old, the fire of God.

Heart Service Greater than Skilled Service

This text is upon the subject of consecration, although the word "consecrate" is not mentioned in it at all; but the word "present," coupled with the word "sacrifice," furnishes us a term that is even stronger in its significance than the word consecrate, and it includes that. You are called upon to present yourself a sacrifice. The word originated in the Old Testament. The victim was brought to the altar, was slain and flayed and laid upon the altar and the blood ran down. You come to the altar and place yourself there. You are not slain, but willing to be slain; you are conformable unto His death. You are not flayed, but willing to be flayed. You may not bleed, but are willing to bleed for Him who bled for you. Every drop of your blood is consecrated to God, so

THE GREAT TRANSACTION 111

that if God needs a martyr, He knows where to find him. You do not court persecution, you do not seek a martyr's death; but you can claim a martyr's crown, because he that thus presents himself to God is made of the stuff of which martyrs are made. You may never have occasion to die for Him who died for you, but God wants to know that it is in you to do it. Someone says, "I doubt if He knows that of any man; I doubt if any man's experience will strike that deep." Someone else says, "Every one has his price"; and another says that it would be a rare, even an impossible, thing to find an individual so intimately devoted to God that before he would stretch forth his hand and betray his trust, he would be struck dead in his track. Maybe they are scarce. Let us assume that there are not many. For the sake of a little investigation, let us assume that there is only one; that somewhere in the world there is one person who measures up to that sort of a loyalty; who would die before he would betray his trust; one whom God could trust anywhere. We will agree for a few unpleasant moments that there is none exepting this one, somewhere in the world. What do you think the Lord has to say about this one? The heavenly Father has the finest sense of appreciation, and will not fail to maintain a proper estimate of such a servant. He has no doubt spoken to the angels about him. Having looked to and fro in the earth for men with hearts perfect toward him, he has that man marked. No matter if he is educated or ignorant, no matter whether he is white or brown, no matter whether he is honored by society or unknown, God has His eye on that man. I think He has charged even the forces of nature with regard to him. I think the Lord participates, in a peculiar way, in the dispensations of that man's life. The obscurity of the man would not govern God's appreciation of him, nor would the limitations of his talent. An earthly syndicate would appreciate such a man as this, if they had a way of knowing that his heart was perfect toward them; and when their fellow syndicates would come to visit them they would refer to him with pride, saying, "That man would die for us; we could trust all the millions of this corporation in his hands. And we appreciate him. If he should die, every wheel of machinery would stop in this plant and we would all stand in sorrow by his grave."

It would be a great advantage for us to have such a wonderful friendship, and to be so estimated at the hand of the heavenly Father. Indeed it would appear to be such a practical thing for one to aspire to this standard of devotion to God that no one would call it fanatical. This is entire consecration.

THE GREAT TRANSACTION 113

THE MORE EXCELLENT CONSECRATION

But someone says, I know every Christian is thus consecrated. No, they do not say it thoughtfully. Sometimes we open our mouths without any particular regard to our judgment and say it. We say every Christian is consecrated, and that is true; but there is a degree and kind of consecration into the depths of which some of us have not gone, and for which some of us are not prepared; when we do come to those terms and commit ourselves to that order of consecration, we are going to get some remarkable revelations of God in our souls.

The consecration set forth in Romans 12:1, 2, is reasonable, but not ordinary. It differs, as to kind, from the attitude which we call consecration in the first stages of the Christian life; it differs also as to degree. The earlier kind of consecration with which the heart is familiar has no well-defined object, this side of gaining heaven; but the *kind* discussed here is for the definite purpose of reaching a deeper experience in the knowledge of God. It is therefore not likely to be made until the individual feels the need of this more complete salvation, and is also made acquainted with the divine provision to supply that need. How soon that will be after conversion depends upon the doctrinal circumstances of his conversion, upon the kind of spiritual leadership he has afterward, and the diligence with which he walks in the light and seeks to fulfil his calling. In the earlier consecration, God cannot always make an unlimited draft upon us. Unconsciously, we have boundaries, and place limitations upon Him to whom the consecration is made. It is made with a generally understood view as to what is expected of us. But this entire consecration is for any use. We become like the ox on the Grecian coin, that stood between the plow and the altar; ready to suffer or to serve.

The word "sacrifice" is synonymous for a *degree* of consecration which leaves nothing off the altar and no price unpaid. It originates in the types of the Old Testament, and it means that the object thus committed to the Lord may be slain. It means, indeed, that we become ready to die for Him that died for us. A sacrifice is that extent of consecration which makes us ready for the worst. A man ready for the worst will be pleasantly disappointed if he gets something less than the worst. If your consecration is such that you could have your physical head cut off for Christ, you will feel that you are quite fortunate if you only have your political or social or ecclesiastical head cut off. If you are so consecrated to Christ that you are willing to be beaten with a cat-o-nine tails for His sake, you will feel that you have gotten off pretty light if you receive nothing but a tongue lashing.

THE GREAT TRANSACTION 115

A man thus consecrated to Christ does not spend much time in complaining about the sufferings and trials that come to him in the world. When a man lives on the mountain top of full consecration, he does not feel like going about and saying, "See what a hard time I am having; the church discounts me, and the community looks down on me; just see what a sufferer I am." He does not pity himself or feel himself in need of sympathy.

The Apostle Paul suffered more than any of us; but he rejoiced always, even when in the shadow of Nero's block. One time, for a special purpose, he recited some of his trials: Once was I stoned, thrice was I beaten with rods, five times received I forty stripes save one. Then he tells some of his experiences on the deep and among wild beasts and among false brethren. Somebody says, "Paul, you have had a hard time; your afflictions have been very heavy." Indeed he was somewhat marred in his body on this account, but you could not get him to pity himself. With the brightness of joy in his countenance, he answers, "Our light affliction, which is but for a moment, worketh for us a far more exceeding and eternal weight of glory." The land where he lived, the land of entire consecration, to which he invites you and me in the appeal of this text, was not a land of murmuring and complaining. It was a mountain top where the sun shines even when earthly clouds hang low.

"I can see far down the mountain,
　Where I wandered weary years,
Often hindered in my journey,
　By the ghosts of doubts and fears;
Broken vows and disappointments
　Thickly sprinkled all the way,
But the Spirit led, unerring,
　To the land I hold to-day.

"Oh, the Cross has wondrous glory!
　Oft I've proved this to be true;
When I'm in the way so narrow
　I can see a pathway through;
And how sweetly Jesus whispers;
　Take the Cross, thou needst not fear,
For I've tried this way before thee,
　And the glory lingers near."

Your bodies are to be presented holy; that is, so far as you are able to make yourself holy. Dedicated, as clean as you can make them. You must do your part so far as you know. One great teacher of this subject in the eighteenth century remarked that if we retrench the superfluities of the flesh, it would prepare the way for God to retrench the superfluities of the soul, which He would do accordingly.

THE GREAT TRANSACTION 117

Our Part May Be Understood

"This is your reasonable service." Paul was a reasoner. He learned his logic from Aristotle, and it is a remarkable fact that while Aristotle's logic has been amplified by modern expressions and illustrations, it has never been essentially improved upon. Paul did not drop this word reasonable in for a punctuation; he dropped it in for the purpose of impressing the readers that so far in the transaction, it was subject to human analysis. It would be approved as a good transaction by any capable business man who took the pains to look seriously into its terms. But when you have gone that far, you have gone so far as human hands can handle the situation. You English grammarians know the meaning of voice as a quality in grammar. You will observe the active voice in the first verse of our chapter and the passive voice in the second. In the first he says, "I beseech you, therefore, brethren, that ye present your bodies a living sacrifice, holy, acceptable unto God;" the act is yours. And then in the next verse, where the passive voice occurs, he says, "Be not conformed to this world: but be ye transformed by the renewing of your mind, that ye may prove what is that good, and acceptable, and perfect, will of God." You are to be passive and in other hands now; another power takes hold of you. He represents the brethren to whom he is speaking as standing in a state of nonconformity to the world. He advises them that they must be on the move, and implies that they will be on the move in one direction or the other. It is a striking fact that in spiritual affairs there is no standing still. A man in grace is like a man on a bicycle; if he stops, he falls. You are going, everlastingly going, somewhere, when it comes to spiritual things. He represents the believer as standing in a state of nonconformity to the world, and in a position to do one of two things: to be conformed to the world, or to be transformed by a certain kind of renewing which is available through entire consecration; which, in other words, becomes a fact when without reserve we abandon ourselves in God's hands and become passive, as clay in the hands of the potter.

"Prove Me, Saith the Lord"

When this, our part, is done, we have got past the reasoning and have come to the part of the transaction which defies analysis. Just here we may observe why many people stop a little too soon, and never enter the fulness. It is because they are not willing to go on in the thing beyond where they can feel their way by the functions of argument or logic. They finish their part *excepting* that they do not guard the offering till the fire falls (see Genesis 15:6-17).

THE GREAT TRANSACTION 119

There are three ways of proving things. You can prove them by *witnesses;* but the proof by witnesses is seldom conclusive. The matter thus set before us may be convincing, and it may lend a great deal of conviction to our hearts as we hear a good man who is sensible and consistent, tell what God has done for him. But at best the proof is incomplete, for it remains that any witness may misinterpret his own experience; and though the testimony be beautiful and consistent, one who is cautious about committing himself may feel that the last word has not yet been said, in the matter of proof.

The second way of proof is by the *authorities.* What I mean by that is the standard text books of interpretation, or those teachers who have made the subject a life study. We go to the standards of our Church, to our creeds, or our best writers and preachers, and say, I want the truth with regard to this matter under consideration. You have specialized in theology and Scripture interpretation, and I want you to make me sure of my ground. You may thus get a great deal of help; but there is one trouble about proving a thing by the authorities; that is, the authorities are so fallible that they sometimes conflict with each other. They are so subject to the temperature around them and to the effect of their own sentiments and the color of their own experience that you may find yourself bewildered by the element of personal equation when you come to compare the statements of the several authorities. Yet they are very helpful. It is the Scriptural way, that we should permit ourselves to be taught; God has ordained some pastors and teachers, and given them the gift. If He has called and qualified some to teach, He must have called some to be taught. So there is nothing wrong in submitting yourself to human teachers. But in the deeper themes of full salvation, we have to be very discriminate in choosing who that teacher shall be, and then allow for his peculiarities and equations. The evidence on a subject like this will always remain a little incomplete if we are forced to rely exclusively on "the authorities" for proof.

The third way of proving the thing is quite different from any other. Most of you have heard what is the proof of the pudding. You all know that the proof of the pudding is not the complexion of the cook, nor the temperature of the oven, nor is it the formula found in the cook book. It is the experimental proof; the proof that comes by placing ourselves in touch with the subject and finding in our own selves an answer to the index. This kind of proof is not possible in all questions, but it is, in the subject before us. The challenge of the Apostle Paul is simply this. I have laid down the terms of consecration, and entreated you to meet them. When you have met them another power will take hold of you and you will be borne on to

THE GREAT TRANSACTION 121

an evidence; you will "prove what is that good, and acceptable and perfect will of God."

THE CHALLENGE

Suppose I should proceed to preach to you upon the laws of electricity, and you were from a country where it has never been applied. You are incapable of understanding all the possibilities which I elaborate upon. I tell you it will shock a man or send a thrill through him if he will place himself in contact with it. You say, "That seems very plausible, but it might be a fellow's imagination." I show you a book on electricity, and you say, It is true that we are taught so in the book, but there must be some misunderstanding. But, having a plate of brass on the floor, connected with a battery, I invite you to stand on it. That is a very simple process of proof. All you have to do is to stand on the plate and see if the teaching is true or not. You thus verify the other forms of proof. When we present to you this full salvation through the blood of Jesus Christ and the fire of the Holy Spirit, one of the most provable of all contentions, even by both the two former methods, we have a right to challenge you to stand upon the plate; to get upon the altar of entire consecration as laid down in this passage and stay there. It is a good proposition, an intelligent transaction. If you make it with a view to being conformed to His image and proving His will, He will meet you on these terms, and you shall know a fact that cannot be reduced to words. Those who will not accept this challenge cannot consistently object that the message is incorrect.

I have often wondered why more have not. It pays, it pays such great dividends. I suppose with some it is because they have a great deal of personal charm and talent, and some might have to sacrifice prospects of promotion. To some of us this complete consecration might seem like losing our individuality and forfeiting the right to control our own affairs; but when you make the transaction and look down on your little pile, it is a pretty shabby looking prospect. I do not enjoy hearing a man tell of what he has given up, as if his inheritance among them that are sanctified by faith had forced him to descend to a lower position. I have a spiritual biography which makes me perhaps peculiarly averse to such talk. You may depend on it that you will get all the friends you need; you will get all the wealth you need; you will get all the position you need. It is entirely possible that the Lord may not agree with worldly arbiters as to what you need, but you will prefer His will. Your ability to make this consecration is not determined by the astuteness of your intellect and it will not depend on the breadth of your education or the perfection

THE GREAT TRANSACTION

of your physical frame; it will depend on the loyalty of your heart.

GUARD THE OFFERING AND PRAY

You get on the altar to remain forever. God knows if you are putting yourself up there for an experiment; He knows when it is only a make believe proposition, for He sees down into your heart. Some events of entire consecration have had their genuineness tested by threatening shadows, such as Abraham's experience in the 15th of Genesis would illustrate when he drove away the threatening vultures that sought to devour the sacrifice, and waited, even into the hour of darkness, for the fire of God to descend upon his offering. But two things, though they be unexpressed, must be understood, when we heed Paul's exhortation; the sincerity of the worshipper may be subjected to a test, and the answer of transforming power must be preceded by prayer. Through prayer is God's way of fulfilling His promises. These two points conceded, and the sacrifice will go upon the altar in good faith, a living sacrifice; and when this is done God will take it; and when He does, let me tell you, my brother, we have not words in our vocabulary to explain what will happen. "Eye hath not seen, nor ear heard, neither hath entered into the heart of man, the things which God hath prepared for them that love Him."

VII

THE VICARIOUS TRAGEDY

Based on John 3:16

"For God so loved the world, that he gave his only begotten Son, that whosoever believeth in him should not perish, but have everlasting life."

"THE world" which God so loved is the entire human race; and the gift of His Son in the capacity here described, implies that in the estimation of God, the world was in a seriously bad fix. This was a fact then; and, to the discerning observer, it continues to be a fact, which should be faced candidly. We should not let any kind of fallacy soften our estimate of the gravity of sin; the reality of the fall of man and the seriousness of his condition. Christ was speaking to Nicodemus, a representative of the Jews, who had not seen a program much more than large enough to include the Province of Palestine. But in this interview, at the close of the first year of His ministry, the Master contemplates a program that goes far beyond the boundaries of Palestine; that stops nowhere short of every human being. God had in mind all the nations of the world when He gave His only begotten Son to make atonement for the sins of men.

A Life Laid Down

The early Church received from Christ, and we receive from the early Church, a cue of exclusiveness which sometimes in our sectarianism we have carried to improper extremes, and into which we may have introduced too many elements; but certainly there are some elements of exclusiveness in the assumptions of the gospel, on which we cannot be broad, as the world defines that term, without self destruction. Christianity never accepted the place offered it in the Pantheon by the broad minded Cæsars; it could not compromise with other gods. It held to the exclusive principle that there is no other name under heaven given among men whereby we must be saved, but Jesus Christ. It is also exclusive in its statement of God's method for evangelizing the world; that is, that He does not propose to evangelize the world through the ministry of angels or through the agency of natural forces, but through the instrumentality of man. Christianity in its best expression understands this to be true, and it is not waiting for something to turn up among the economic or political forces to solve the problem of world evangelization, nor is it waiting for some decree to come from the Almighty, through which, by fiat, the human race shall come to a knowledge of salvation. On this point it is exclusive. The Christianity which survived the trials of the early centuries, and the Christianity which is destined to exist when all other kinds of Christianity have become numbered with the curio of history, is the Christianity which holds to the necessity of the suffering and death and resurrection of Jesus Christ, in God's economy for the salvation of man; which does not for a moment assume, in view of this economy, that there could have been any other way for making possible the salvation of a human being. The Scriptures are very definite upon that fact. For instance, in Acts 17:3 the Apostle Paul says that "Christ must needs have suffered, and risen from the dead" to make possible this program of evangelism; and in Hebrews 9:16 it is said, "Where a testament is, there must also of necessity be the death of the testator." The Gospels are replete in their reference to the absolute necessity of the suffering and death and resurrection of Christ. We may understand this thought to have been in the Master's mind when He made the remark to Nicodemus that, "God so loved the world that He gave His only begotten Son that whosoever believeth in Him should not perish, but have everlasting life."

THE VICARIOUS TRAGEDY 127

RIGHT IS RIGHT FOREVER

There is implied in this passage the fact of judgment, of penalty for sin. The sad alternative is that if men do not receive the benefit of salvation voluntarily, through our Lord Jesus Christ, they are destined not to get into heaven; they are destined to come to some bad end as a consequence of broken law; they are destined to perish, whatever that means; to be lost, whatever that means; to be turned into hell, whatever that means. In its principle, law has no beginning. Older than ancient mountains or tables of stone, it resides in the nature of God. Upon its framework the whole universe is builded. If an angel in the midst of heaven's glory should stand upon an order of God, if, when God said to him, Do this, the angel would say, I will not do it, he would find himself in collision with immutable law. Of course we cannot conceive of such a thing taking place. It is the universal assumption that the day of probation has ended with the angels. But if we could imagine such a thing, we must realize that the angel would bring infinite calamity upon himself.

Law cannot be law without penalty. A law without a penalty is only a piece of advice or suggestion. It deserves to be called law in proportion as the penalty for its transgression is sure. But a penalty must be commensurate only with the seriousness of the offense; no more, no less. If the government of a nation should enact a law providing that anyone who killed a magistrate of that nation should be fined five dollars, you would regard it as absurd. If they should enact a law providing that any who broke open sealed letters in custody of the government should have their necks broken, we should consider it an outrage. But I wish to call your attention to the fact that there is no trifling violation of divine law. Offenses against God are never small; for in every such offense there is a principle which would dethrone the Almighty and undo His government. Sin is to be estimated in the light of its highest possible development, not in the light of its mere elementary expression. You are not to soften your estimate of sin in proportion with its simplicity, its seeming respectability, or its apparent convenience; but you are to judge it by the virus which is in the very nature of sin itself; those strange, weird laws which make for its immeasurable possibilities. These laws inhere in sin wherever you find it.

Adam's Imitators

That was a small offense which Adam committed in the garden of Eden, as told in Genesis. The transaction seems to be very simple, but you are not to estimate the gravity of his

THE VICARIOUS TRAGEDY 129

sin by the single transaction as given us in the record. Adam was not in a position to realize fully how serious was his offense against God. If he could read the morning papers now, and go about and view some of the scenes of affliction and suffering, and the terrible orgies of death, he would realize in a greater measure what a serious transaction that was on his part when he took it upon himself to sin against God. Let us illustrate. Here is a man standing by the railroad track some miles from the city. It is eleven o'clock in the evening. The moon is shining. He looks at his watch and estimates that within ten minutes the great through train with a load of excursionists will be passing that way, and he resolves to wreck the train. Going down to the spur, he takes out a key, throws open the switch, and stands back to see what will happen. The train comes through at forty miles an hour and leaps out on the side track; the coaches pile, one on top of another, flames shoot up from the wreckage, and the cry of a perishing multitude is heard. Fortunately there was a circumstance by which this man was apprehended on the spot, and carried to the station where the people were waiting to meet their friends who were coming on the train. The people felt that capital punishment was too good for the man who, cruelly and in cold blood, had taken in his hands the lives of their loved ones. But let us suppose that when this man stood back among the trees to see the tragedy, just as the train approached, a good man who had been standing under the shadow of a tree on the other side and had seen the switch opened, had rushed in and turned it back, and the train has passed in safety, the passengers unconscious of their danger. In that case the one who opened the switch would not have been such a wicked man, in the eyes of human justice; he would not have been condemned so seriously; but in the eyes of divine justice, he would be the same sinful monster in either case. It was not to his credit that the good man closed the switch and prevented the tragedy; it therefore subtracted nothing from his guilt.

Some man may say, Yes, I commit sins that look as large as Adam's sin; but I do not stand at the head of a great race; there are circumstances connected with me and limitations in me that prevent my sin producing such a terrible influence. But you are not to be credited for your altered environment; you are to be judged in the light of the highest possible development of your sin. If you are to be judged according to the gravity of your guilt, how great is that judgment to be. It cannot be measured. I may say advisedly that sin is infinite in its possibilities. If the race could go on multiplying forever, and there were no redeeming mercy or reclaiming agencies, sin would prove to be infinite in its possibilities. I think,

THE VICARIOUS TRAGEDY 131

therefore, we are reasonable in concluding that the guilt of sin is infinite. Sometimes in opposing the doctrine of the future doom of the lost, a critic will say, "How could a finite being be infinitely cast off or punished?" But it looks as though a finite being might be infinitely guilty; it therefore follows that an extenuation of hell must be sought elsewhere than at the bar of justice. Your guilt is not measured by your stature or the magnitude of your intellect. While you and I are fallible, there are some things which we infallibly know. Among those things, we know, at least in a few instances, what is right and what is wrong. We know it so well, notwithstanding our imperfections and frailties, that it would be impossible for an angel in heaven to know it better; and we can commit sin, we can commit great sin. Great sins are not to be recognized according to their enormity, and great sinners are not to be estimated according to their stature; that was the schoolboy's idea of greatness, when he said,

"How big was Alexander, Pa, that people call him great; was he like old Goliath tall, his spear a hundred weight?"

But the father gave him to understand that stature was not the measure of greatness, when he replied, "Not so, my son, about as large as I or Uncle James." It was not the stature of the man, nor the weight of his sword, that made him great; it was the number of men he killed.

You can be just as great a sinner in the sight of God and be five feet high, as you could if you were five miles high. You can be as great a sinner and quite as guilty before the divine judgment with a weak arm, not strong enough to unhinge the front door of a church, as you could be if you were strong enough to endanger the walls of the new Jerusalem. If you were as large as the American continent, and tall enough to step over seas, from one continent to another; if you were so great that you could move with head among the stars and reach up and pluck them out of the skies; so terrible that angels would feel it necessary to get out of your way; if you were large enough to be a veritable rival to the Almighty on His throne, you would not be more guilty than you are at five feet high. You might be much more dangerous; but your guilt is not measured by the amount of harm you are capable of doing. Despite your relative helplessness, your sin is as serious before the bar of divine justice as if you were a prodigy of strength and greatness; as serious as was Adam's sin in Eden after God had said, "In the day thou eatest thereof thou shalt surely die."

What Wondrous Love

The verdict was in advance. When Adam sinned, Justice already stood with her sword sus-

THE VICARIOUS TRAGEDY

pended, ready to cut him off; but God stayed the hand of Justice and said, "Wait, I love him;" then Justice said, "Though God's love is great, He cannot lie; and God has said that the sinner must surely die." But God said, "Wait; when I planned in the councils of heaven to make him, I loved him; when I formed the earth for his habitation and divided the waters and the land, I loved him; when I planted the Garden eastward in Eden, I loved him; when I walked with him and communed with him in the cool of the day, I loved him." In the midst of that tragic situation, the great God devised a scheme so profound that the angels have looked into it with admiration; so wonderful that no human mind has ever yet analyzed the depths of its wisdom. That scheme was the atonement in Jesus Christ. The finite mind can only apprehend a few manifest facts connected with the plan of redemption; but these are sufficient for us to enjoy its benefits ourselves and publish the same to others. It was when God contemplated this situation that he made provision for the marvelous sacrifice described in John 3:16.

Not only has the merit of that atonement cleared the way, under the government analogy, for man's return to God; but with this provision for his justification, his recovery to the divine favor, it provides automatically for his adoption and regeneration; it provides under further conditions, for his entire sanctification and for his ultimate redemption, faultless, before the throne; it provides potentially for every need that falls upon his being; for "He that spared not his own Son, but delivered him up for us ALL, how shall he not with him also freely give us ALL things."

Two Parties to the Transaction

"If," says one, "the atonement in Christ was made for the world, we shall all be saved; if God gave His Son to make possible the salvation of every man, and if He died for all men, as plainly stated in the Scriptures, all men shall be saved." But that does not follow at all; salvation in Christ is conditional; and you will permit me to exhort you to guard jealously, and study with devout concern, the conditions of salvation. The words "whosoever believeth" imply that every man who is saved must have chosen Christ, must have chosen salvation in Christ, and all that goes with it in the way of obedience and repentance. Let me illustrate this with an improvised picture. There lived a man in the eastern part of America who was well known throughout his state. He raised a group of splendid children, who were instructed in his own splendid ideals. But among the number he had one son who was the black sheep of the flock. This boy repudiated the instruc-

THE VICARIOUS TRAGEDY 135

tions of his father, and went away from home, into the far west, connecting himself with a community of anarchists in the Rocky Mountains and engaged in robbery and murder. Finally, the authorities of California got hold of him; and, though through a technicality he escaped the gallows, he was sentenced to the penitentiary to work at hard labor, for life. Such was his reputation that the warden required him to wear a ball and chain. From here he wrote his first letter home. It was tear-stained. He told his father about the grim prison walls, the scantiness of his food, and the hopelessness of his condition. When the father received that letter, he said, "At last our son's proud spirit is broken and he is humbled; I thank God that I have hope for him yet." The father went to the Supreme Justice and other officials of his state, obtained the finest recommendations possible, and took the fastest train for California, making his appeal in person to the governor of that State. He was received with great courtesy, and allowed to present his plea for the pardon of his son, which he based upon the standing and condition of his family. After the plea was over, the governor said, "I cannot grant the pardon; your son was a great offender against the State, barely escaping capital punishment. Being under oath to defend the laws of this commonwealth and uphold its courts, I cannot take it upon myself to grant him pardon." But the father was a resourceful man, and with great eloquence, enriched with a broken heart, he continued his plea, putting himself in the governor's place and the governor in his place, till finally the governor's judgment was convinced and his heart moved. He took from his desk two documents and inscribed and signed them, and handed them to the father, saying, "Go and have your son read both of these, and sign them formally in the presence of witnesses, and he shall be free." The father was received with courtesy at the prison by the warden. Going into the cell where his son was kept, they sat down and rejoiced together in tears, that all the provisions for his release had been made. The son read and signed the first document, which was a bill of pardon, formally indicted by the governor of the State, to be received by the son through merely adding his signature. It was a very simple transaction. It is a simple transaction to get your sins forgiven, when you present yourself to God. The full provision is already made, the pardon only waits your voluntary acceptance, through simple faith. But there was another document for the son to read and sign before he could have his pardon. It was an oath of allegiance to the federal government and to the laws of California. As he read this, his face became agitated and an angry look flashed in his eye. He began to reflect aloud on the unfairness of one man or a group

THE VICARIOUS TRAGEDY 137

of men putting up standards for other men, and to rant upon the doctrines of anarchism. At last, falling into a fury, he gathered up the two documents, tore them to pieces, and, clanking his chains, went back into the rear of his cell and sat there in the darkness, glaring like a mad dog. His father went away from the prison with a sad heart. Do you suppose he went back to the governor and said, "You made the conditions too hard; if you would make my son's pardon unconditional, we could save him; but as long as you attach a condition to his pardon, it will be impossible for us to take him out of prison. He did nothing of the kind. He went to the station and took a train for home. He went home with a broken heart, but he went approving every judgment of the courts of California, affirming that his son was exactly where he ought to be.

CONSISTENT TEARS

Somebody says, "When I come to the Judgment, and the wicked are placed upon the left and the righteous upon the right, and the righteous are received into the everlasting Kingdom and the wicked banished from the presence of God, if I have loved ones lost, my heart shall be broken, it will be impossible to reconcile me; it will be difficult for them to make me happy in heaven." That seems true from our viewpoint, not weighing the fact that this loved one has refused to accept the laws of the Kingdom in repentance and faith, has refused to follow Christ, and has taken it upon himself to reject salvation, except as God should be willing to give him salvation *in his sins*. But you are going to see the justice of the judgment of God as clearly as this father saw the justice of the law when he left his son in the state prison. It will be natural for you to have sorrow, as this father did. There is only one thing that can keep you from being sad in that day, and that will be a miracle of God; but that will take place. It is implied that the multitude of the redeemed shall come weeping to the gates, when it is said that God shall wipe away all tears from their eyes. Just here many a person has been drawn into a false belief which makes no provision for the wisdom that safeguards the law of God, which makes no provision for the divine sovereignty and the integrity of heaven. They have turned to some kind of sentimental doctrine of second probation or new theology in order to comfort their souls with a delusion that their loved ones will somehow be saved, without meeting the conditions of repentance and subscribing to the laws of the kingdom of heaven. But there is no use to console one's self with a positive error. We cannot modify stern facts by becoming exercised over fond opinions. "But," one says, "I cannot bear to

THE VICARIOUS TRAGEDY 139

see them lost; if I should see them lost, my heart would be wrung and I should weep with bitter weepings." You are bearing it now, often with most inadequate concern, and we must remind you that the soul of your loved one is as truly lost as it will be a million years from now. He may not be as miserably lost, he may not be as consciously lost, he may not be as hopelessly lost, as he will be a million years from now; but he is as really lost, and must continue to be lost, until he is saved through the atonement of Jesus Christ. Are you worrying about it now? It will do you no good when you come to that great day of separation between the righteous and the wicked for you then to weep and worry; it will do you a great deal of good to be concerned about it now. It will do them much good for you to be concerned about them now. Tears in the judgment will be futile. Weeping and wailing when men have sealed their doom will be in vain; but tears of concern and solicitude and pleas of intercession, do a vast amount of good today.

The Vision and the Burden

No one has ever measured the possibilities of soul winning on the part of the individual that loves God, who has a clear enough conception of faith to accept these great future events as realistically as if already present, and who does not wait until their fulfillment to let them affect him, but who lets them affect him now; and who, on the strength of this great contemplation, sets about helping his fellow beings while it will do some good. If you have the vision, it will break your heart, not only to see your loved ones, but to see any people cut off from God and perishing; and if you want to be saved from some very sad regrets when you stand before the judgment seat of Christ, the thing for you to do is to point them *now* to the Lamb of God that taketh away the sin of the world.

In the passage we have examined, it is shown:

That no evils coming upon man can be attributed to a limit in God's love, for it has no limit;

That there must be a fearful meaning to the doctrine that man is lost, since such a great price is paid to make his salvation possible;

That all enlightened beings are doomed, unless voluntarily, with consistent purpose, they seek salvation through the atonement of Christ;

That only a great salvation will do, and that nothing less than a great salvation should be expected, in view of the greatness of Him who comes to save us;

That God's love and its saving provision, is without respect of persons or races, so that we can feel free to offer the benefits of a full gospel to all mankind.

VIII

"MY CUP"

BASED ON PSALM XXIII

"He restoreth my soul."

IN this Psalm we have the testimony of another of the Old Testament authorities who, by a stalwart faith, advanced ahead of their time in spiritual things and partook of a measure of personal salvation somewhat similar to that which is generally provided through the Gospel. There is, in a remarkable measure, a New Testament atmosphere in several of the Psalms. In this instance, by the use of a line of fascinating imagery, the Psalmist tells what the Lord is to him and what the Lord does for him. Starting out deliberately, he refers to Jehovah in the second person, as his shepherd, doing certain things for him; but as he warms up in the testimony, the consciousness of the Divine presence becomes so imperative that he proceeds to address the Lord in the first person: "Yea, though I walk through the valley of the shadow of death, I will fear no evil: for THOU art with me; THY rod and THY staff, they comfort me."

The fundamental testimony in this Psalm of the inner life is in the words, "He restoreth my soul." Around that profession all the thoughts of the testimony seem to revolve. It is the central idea of his profession; and, rudimentally, it is that same religious experience to which a certain eminent writer refers as the central idea of Christianity. The word "restore" is the same as that used in the instance where the Master healed the man with the withered hand. It was explained that the hand, being "restored," was "whole as the other"; that is, it was like a hand ought to be; a normal hand. The standard of salvation provided in both the Old and New Testament is one which, through the grace of God, recovers the soul from its fallen condition; from its condemned estate and from its moral diseases, into a normal state, making it what a soul ought to be.

Soul Sickness

Restore is a health term; we may take it to mean, in this instance, that the individual is well in his soul. There is such a thing as soul disease; it is no mere figure of speech. Just as certainly as a man may have rheumatism in his body, he may have pride and vanity in his soul. Just as he may have malignant out-

"MY CUP"

breakings from disease of his blood and skin, he may have an ugly temper and a mean disposition; and that ugly temper or mean disposition resides in his spiritual nature. It is so far removed from anything like a scientific analysis, so entirely spiritual and exceedingly subtle that if anyone should attempt to approach it, as a materialistic investigator, he could never locate it. It is not available through the microscope or by the most delicate instrument of science. You may take a man that has that ugly disposition in him, and have at his side another man with a good disposition; yet they could be the same complexion, and have the same hereditary traits in their physical being, they could be the same weight, and their bodies could represent exactly the same chemical properties in every respect; physical dispositions alike, with moral dispositions as far apart as the north pole and the equator. It matters not how minute might be the physical research, the difference in these men could not be explained in histology, because the trouble is in the soul. Nor is this disease of the soul available for the student of psychology. Some man, recently writing on Sunday School pedagogy, said that modern psychology had discovered there was no such thing as hereditary depravity. Such writers forget, if they have ever learned, that modern psychology calls itself the science of consciousness; and, as such, operates sparingly in the realm of metaphysics and theology, and always with great modesty. Soul disease is the only explanation of the fact that man is singular among all other living creatures in showing a universal tendency to violate the laws of his being from his earliest coordinations. Its mode of existence can no more be demonstrated by mental science than by physical science. We know it is present only when it manifests itself or when the Spirit of God reveals it. But be sure of this, there is such a thing as soul disease. So far is "Christian Science" mistaken in its refusal of a place to any disease in the realm of reality, there are diseases both physical and spiritual; and the latter reality is quite as stubborn as the former. It is the duty of the pulpit to reckon with this latter fact and to find the remedy.

The Progeny of Satan

What is the restoration of the soul? We may safely say it is one and the same thing with full salvation from all sin, for the simple reason that the definition of sin properly stated does not include any materialistic conception. It used to be thought otherwise. Christianity, in the early centuries of the era became mixed up with Neoplatonism and Gnosticism and got its notion of sin confused. In a less favored period, some theologians worked this old idea to the limit; and some have not yet discovered

"MY CUP"

that we have outgrown the fallacy. The idea was that sin is a trouble of the flesh, a material something, that inheres in the physical man. The theory of the old heathen gnostic from whom we imbibed this tincture of philosophy, was that all material had sin in it; every grain of sand, all the dust of the ground, and, therefore, all the trees that grow out of the ground and all the fruit that grows on the trees and all the grass that grows in the field, and all the cattle that feed on the grass, are sinful in proportion to their material bulk. They held accordingly that inasmuch as man, in his physical being, assimilates these things, he is all sin. The outcome of the philosophy, to be consistent, was that man's merit and demerit should be determined by the length of his girdle and the amount of avoirdupois which he represented; the logic of it is that a man who is emaciated is accordingly a saint, and a man who is so unfortunate as to be corpulent and stout is decidedly sinful. This theory of sin has no place in common sense and no support in the Scriptures. Were it true, full salvation from sin in this life would be an illogical doctrine; with this old error as a premise, the advocate of full deliverance from sin in this life could be nothing less than a fanatic; nor could there be any hope of full deliverance from sin except by the aid of the graveyard. Then death would be a friend and not an enemy.

I wish to call your attention to the fact that the carnal mind is mind, not matter; so, when David in his testimony professed full restoration, he professed it not for his body but for his soul; saying of Jehovah, "He restoreth my soul." It was neither here nor there with his body; nor is it here or there with my body, nor was it with Paul's body. It had its appetites, its infirmities, and its imperfections. He found it necessary to take care of it and to control it; and he said he was making a success of the job. "I keep my body under," said he. The idea that this vehicle which our soul inhabits is a sinful thing, should be discarded as unworthy the intelligence of an enlightened people. It can be consecrated to God, but positive holiness is a thing of the soul, because sin is a thing of the soul. Sin may exercise itself through our physical faculties, if it resides in the soul; and in this exercise it may seem very much as though the body itself were the sinner; but the manifestation of sin in our physical being is the action of mind upon matter; for sin is spiritualistic in its origin, its author and progenitor, a spiritual agent, being unable to produce a physical entity.

Heaven's Overtures

There are three manifest stages in the restoration of the soul, all of which are divine, for

"MY CUP"

God does the restoring. This is recognized in the testimony, "*He* restoreth my soul." The three stages which are therefore supernaturally produced, are, Conviction, and Regeneration, the giving of spiritual life, and Holiness or the giving of spiritual health. Keep clear the fact that each stage is wholly and exclusively divine. We grant that there is a human side to it; but the part that we perform, of repentance, obedience, prayer, consecration, trust, can not, in any fraction, accomplish the thing in us, but simply puts us in the place where God can do the work in us.

Conviction is the work of the Holy Spirit. No man could ever move Godward unless the Spirit of God showed that man his sin and opened to him the vision which we call conviction, discovering the possibilities of salvation. We who are working for the evangelization of the world ought to keep that in mind, that we are implicitly dependent upon God's Spirit for Scriptural results; that no argument of ours can make any man feel he is a sinner. It may cause him to admit that he is a sinner, but after his reason is convinced, he will smile and congratulate us for our bright arguments, and walk the streets with perfect complacency. But when God's spirit speaks to him through your lips or through your influence, saying, "Man, you are a sinner," he will clutch at his heart and say, "O God, I know it; but I never felt it to be true so keenly as I do today." There is a great difference between the Spirit of God telling him he is a sinner, and my telling him he is a sinner; and I wish to remind you that the Holy Spirit can and will do this thing; He is in the business of convicting sinners, when we pray and look to Him with this definite object. If we think *We* can do it, and go along with our brilliant arguments and our shining theories and splendid methods of revival work, trying thus to accomplish it, He will let us go on and do it; but if, while we are doing our best, which we certainly ought to do, we keep in mind the fact that all real conviction is a work of the Holy Spirit, entreating Him accordingly, we are likely to have greater results in the form of Scriptural conviction, which is stage number one in the restoration of the soul.

Stage two is the regeneration of the soul, or bringing a man spiritually from death to life. The Scriptures recognize that a sinner is dead in sin. This is not merely a figure of speech, it is literally true in a very important sense. Certain sublime faculties lie dormant in the sinner's nature; there are emotions of peace and joy and assurance existent in the heart of a man who is regenerated to which the unregenerated man is a stranger. There are elements of consciousness brought into existence as a result of the Scriptural conversion of a soul which afford real ground for the conclusion that a man in sin is dead and a man regenerate is alive.

"MY CUP"

Falling Short without Falling

All do not agree on the terms of the third stage in the restoration of a soul. Some merge it with the second, some complicate it otherwise. Sometimes they insist that life and health are the same thing; that it would be impossible for a man to be spiritually alive without being spiritually well or every whit whole. But this would destroy the sense of the analogy, render meaningless the assertions of the New Testament, and collide with the stubborn facts of experience. Referring to their neglect of self examination and their improper use of the means of grace, the apostle Paul, in the eleventh of 1st Corinthians, tells the membership of that church that many of them are sickly and weak. In his discussion of the subject of Holiness, which might properly be the title of the twelfth chapter of Hebrews, he refers to the affliction of spiritual lameness. "Lest that which is lame be turned out of the way," he says: "Lift up the hands that hang down and the feeble knees." Thus he refers to the weak Christians who are about to quit praying and battling against evil. He desires that the lame saint be healed. We have all seen lame Christians, and it would be unfair, if because they were lame, we should say they were dead. They are lame in many ways; some perhaps lame in their loyalty to the work of the church; some lame in their veracity in business dealings. Some one asks: "Do you mean to tell me that a converted man will lie?" No, he will not lie; all liars are explicitly unqualified for heaven, according to the Scriptures. Hence, he who lies disproves his claim of conversion; but one may strain the truth without wilfully lying. Some good men, under stress of selfish interest, have told the "truth" so weakly that they were afterward, at the bar of their own conscience, condemned as being lame in their veracity. You might find this health defect indicated in several phases of the ethical life, where the individual, not quite well in his soul, will be found to halt or limp in the way of righteousness. But, happily, we can be healed. The plain promise is before us; and the provision is ample. God is no respecter of persons. He who recovered David from his moral adversities and restored his soul will do the same for every one who repairs unto Him with a passion for righteousness.

Quarreling With Symbols

We have studied the three stages in the restoration of the soul; Conviction, Regeneration, and Health or Holiness. Of the latter it has been said, "You may call it what you please, it does not matter what you call it." We would say, it does not matter what you call it, if it does not matter; but if it matters, it matters.

"MY CUP" 151

That sounds like an ambiguous piece of English; but it means, if in your heart you are prejudiced against a Scriptural term intended to convey the idea of this Christian experience, it would be a very good thing for you to be crucified on that term; that is about the very best term for you to use when you go into your closet to seek the fulness of the blessing, if you are in earnest. "But," you say, "my church calls it so and so;" permit me to recommend the other word for you. I can call it "so and so," but you would do well to call it by the name against which you have formed a prejudice, till you recover from your dislike of that word; for the Spirit of God can hardly do His best work in you so long as He finds in you any antipathy for a Bible term.

Blessings that Flow

Let us next observe what results from the restoration of the soul. A circle of glorious consequences or concomitants is described in the imagery of the Psalmist's testimony. One result is satisfaction. That appears in the first verse. "The Lord is my shepherd, I shall not want." The essence of that profession is, I have found in Him a satisfying portion and my heart has ceased to wander. In any capacity of life, a man is more useful when he is satisfied; a soldier in any army is a more powerful factor when he is satisfied; a complacent citizen in any community is more useful than a ne'er-do-well. And God can use you better as citizens of Zion and as soldiers of the cross, if He can get you sufficiently acquainted with Him that you are able to find in Him a satisfying portion. But you do not have to seek satisfaction as such; only get your soul restored, and Satisfaction will seek you. You cannot get away from her benign presence, though you go deep into the tangles of heathenism.

Consequent upon the restoration of his soul the Psalmist is able to say, "He leadeth me in the paths of righteousness for His name's sake." He uses the plural, paths, indicating that there are certain intricacies connected with living right which it is pretty hard for a man in his own strength to solve. But there is an experience of inward deliverance where we can so associate ourselves with Him as to be practical overcomers in the demands of every day life. Our inward agreement with Him can be such that He can take us by the hand and supplement our frail strength. He has a reason for wanting to do this. You are His representative; His child; through you He gets His reputation in the world. It would be a calamity if you should go about as His child and give Him a bad reputation. He wants you to make a success of practical Christianity. You will have your frailties as long as you live in the world, in the temporal body; but amidst it all, it is possible for you to live a life of victory, and your living thus will mean much. But to do this, you must have special help from heaven. You are not to get this help by seeking it as such; get your soul restored, and this aid to efficiency, this every day help, will be always at hand.

Some people are very anxious about getting the fulness of God, referring to it as something to be received subsequent to heart purity. The Psalmist says in his testimony that he has received it: "My cup runneth over." It is important that we should have this. They tell us that the reason the Nile valley produces such tremendous harvests is because it gets so many overflows. If we had a few more overflowing saints who had blessings to spare, I think this poor old thirsty world around us would get more out of our religion. How do you get the overflow? Get your soul restored and the fulness of the blessing will take care of itself. As there is no vacuum in nature, there is no vacuum in grace; and if you will let God restore your soul, the fulness will not have to be sought as such; it will seek you. Good people often are prone to spend much time going out after great blessings or manifestations when the fact is if God gets us sound and well in our souls, these great blessings and manifestations will come after us instead of our having to go after them. Pray for soul health instead of praying for satisfaction. Get your soul restored, through faith in the blood of Christ, and you will not have to seek blessings. The blessing will go home with you; and when you awaken in the morning it will be at your bedside, and when you go to your work, you will find the blessing there.

We have not time to go over all the things which result from the restoration of the soul; but by following up the same trend of interpretation, you will find a great catalogue of blessings which the Psalmist proves to have received in connection with spiritual restoration. Among them you will find his assurance for the future. He says, "Goodness and mercy shall follow me all the days of my life, and I shall dwell in the house of the Lord forever." It is a comforting thing for a man to have some way of knowing in his own heart every moment that he has his arrangements made for all the future. The most fortunate man in this house tonight is the man with a great future. I do not envy a man who has no future. It matters not how brilliant may be that man's present; or how rich he may be; or how highly favored; it matters not how well surrounded he may be; if that man has no great future, I should be sorry to stand in his shoes. I believe in the man that has a great future, even if his clothes are thread-bare and his shoes are worn out and he is surrounded with poverty. In that he has a great future, I may well envy his lot. Happy is that people with a great future, without any reference to what is

"MY CUP" 155

the present; but happier still are they if they have some kind of guarantee that they have a great future. The Psalmist tells us that he has found that guarantee, and has it with him. If you would find it, do not seek it as such; get your soul restored and it will be yours.

SAVED FROM THE FOG

There is an intuitive element in the Psalmist's faith as a result of the restoration of his soul. He said, "Surely." That is a very pretty word. Did you ever walk around it and size it up? Some people, even leaders, in the religious world, seem to feed upon uncertainties. To express doubt sounds learned to some and modest to others. There are so many things upon which our happiness depends that they think are not to be ascertained. They are not quite sure of the authenticity of the Bible, the deity of Christ, the soul of man, and the facts of the future state. We may safely infer that this is due to a condition of the heart. It is wonderful, when the dross of sin gets into a man's heart, how dim his vision is, and how impotent his imagination may become in regard to these great truths. He is not able to apprehend them, although he be loaded down with proof, his power to perceive evidence on spiritual and eternal themes is impaired. Such men often think their great two-story heads prevent their enjoyment of a simple faith in the orthodox message of the gospel; but they only illustrate the old philosophic truth that sentiment and mood may serve to color a reasoner's premises. You could not cure such men with a head treatment, but we have never seen heart treatment fail. No matter how great a man he was, no matter if he were two or three stories high intellectually; when he bows down before an altar of prayer, gets right with God, and receives the baptism with the Holy Spirit, getting his soul restored, you will no longer hear him talk against the authenticity of the Scriptures, or the deity of Christ, or the necessity for the atonement, or the right views of the future state, or any of those other things without which Christianity would not have survived to this day. A man may have a level head without a clean heart; but full salvation is the only anchor that invariably holds against the storm of "new thought" and destructive criticism. The healthy soul is always able to grasp and realize the truths essential to eternal life.

No one need suppose that the deniers of the orthodox gospel message have any inside information, or that they feel any sort of ultimate assurance that we who preach this message are mistaken. Aside from these convictions peculiar to a restored soul, Macaulay's words apply to all men: "The truth is that no powers of mind constitute a security against errors of this descrip-

"MY CUP" 157

tion. Touching God and His ways with man, the highest faculties human can discover little more than the meanest. In theology the interval is small indeed between Aristotle and a child, between Archimedes and a naked savage." So it is with a natural man, who cannot know things that are spiritually discerned. No knowledge of archæology and the classics can obviate his helplessness.

A gentleman in the midst of Billy Sunday's work in the East, who had his head trouble and did not know how to get rid of it, confessed the superiority of the old gospel when he saw the power of Mr. Sunday's ministry and listened to the stentorian notes of orthodoxy from that John the Baptist of America. Here are his words, written for the *Boston Transcript:* "His (Mr. Sunday's) unmistakable passion for righteousness and the all embracing democracy of his religion which recognized that the lowest drunkard in the gutter and the most sin-seared woman of the town are just as much worth saving, just as precious in the sight of God, as the most respectable member of society made me wish that I could believe his theology." That was a frank response, but there is only one way of effecting a cure when a man's head gets into that fix; there are not enough books in the libraries of the John Wesleys and Charles Finneys to cure his head trouble, but there is one thing that will wonderfully clarify the intricate meditations of a man who is burdened down with such tremendous intellectual findings, and that is for him to get down before God and get this great healing touch upon his soul.

Looking for Stage Four

The Psalmist says he is assured, not only that he will dwell in the house of the Lord forever, but he has assurance for this life also: "Goodness and mercy shall follow me all the days of my life." He personifies Goodness and Mercy, makes them into two angels, and represents them as being on his track; so that if he ever falls into a ditch on the road of life or gets on a dangerous path or otherwise comes to grief, he can rejoice that his troubles shall only be temporary; he is soon to be overtaken by the two angels that follow him, not some of the days, but all the days of his life. He carries in his soul such conviction of security, both with reference to the rear guard and the welcoming committee which awaits him in the beyond, that it gives triumphant poise to all the meditations of his soul. There is nothing that makes for health and serenity of mind and sweet sleep and bright days and glad songs and magnificent contemplations, like having the assurance in your soul that everything is all right; that God is taking care of the past, that the rear guard of divine providence is supporting you, and that you have a mansion in the skies.

IX

SOUL PILOTS

BASED UPON HEBREWS 12:1-15

"For they verily for a few days chastened us after their own pleasure; but he for our profit, that we might be partakers of his holiness."

SCIENCE tells us that there are eight planets revolving around the sun, each describing a circle wider than the other; so that there are eight different circles described by the planets. Up till last century it was thought there were only seven planets; but there began to be a suspicion in the early part of the century that there were eight. The planet Neptune, which is the outer planet, is not visible to the natural eye, and would probably never have been discovered if they had not first suspected that it existed, and begun to hunt for it. For many years, the astronomers had been observing the erratic behavior of Uranus, the most remote of the known planets, which, while all others were true to the law of their calculations, always managed to make some new detour which kept it from making its circuit on schedule time.

This proved to be the gravitative influence of another planet yet undiscovered. Before its discovery, Herschell wrote: "We see it as Columbus saw America from the shores of Spain. Its movements have been felt trembling along the far reaching line of our analysis with a certainty not far inferior to ocular demonstration." They tell us that in 1846 a scientist in France announced the position of the unknown planet and another in England agreed with the calculation. The former wrote to Dr. Galle of Berlin for assistance in searching for the planet, who, with the aid of the large telescope, found it in less than a degree of the place described by the Frenchman in his letter.

Following Our Hearts

After conversion to Christ, there is something in the behavior of the regenerate heart that indicates the need of a more advanced experience of grace. For a long time the Episcopalians and Presbyterians and Methodists and Baptists, and others, have been admitting that there must be a deeper work of grace. This was due to the almost uniform verdict of their own hearts. They all began to seek for it in the Word of God, assuming that God had provided an answer to this manifest need of His children. They were right, and it has been definitely located and its attributes determined in God's Word;

though there are some who do not yet realize that this Neptune has been discovered. In 1729 a little man by the name of John Wesley discovered that we could not be saved without holiness; and 1737, while reading the Scriptures, he saw likewise that men are justified before they are sanctified. This little man did not weigh but one hundred and twenty pounds, yet, he took the telescope of faith and located this Neptune of Christian experience so precisely that unsophisticated men of every denomination, reading the Scriptures with obedient, seeking hearts, have found the answer to their need within a degree of where he charted it in the theological heavens.

The Wesleyan Formula

In his old age, Mr. Wesley collected some of his own writings upon this subject, showing the "steps" of his own progress in the direction of a full apprehension of Christian holiness, up to the year 1775. Since leaders of all denominations regard John Wesley as an epoch making man, it may be in place for us to refer to the elements of his *"grand depositum."* At one stage in his life we find him discovering that we cannot be saved without holiness; at another stage, he is discovering that we are justified before we are sanctified; a little later, his writings show his conviction that it is secured by faith, and is, therefore, an instantaneous work of divine grace. At another stage he is discovering that it is attested by the witness of the Holy Spirit, the same as our justification. Finally, he registers his opinion in 1758 that the experience is forfeitable, that it is possible for a Christian to lose the full salvation blessing out of his heart. He collects these writings into a little volume called "A Plain Account of Christian Perfection"; and nothing that has been written in the many years that have elapsed since that time seems to represent any more advanced information upon this great subject. This little book, without book unity, a mere collation, giving the steps by which he embodied the advanced Christian experience in a definite doctrinal presentation, is now read by Christians of all theological persuasions.

A Proof of the Father's Love

The lesson which we have read discusses a certain kind of chastisement, a chastisement which seeks to secure a special object in the heart of the Christian. This object is indicated in the 10th verse. God chastens men under other circumstances and for other objects. He sometimes chastens the wicked as a matter of judgment; and, sometimes, with a view to bringing them to repentance. Then, if we as Christians become disobedient or refuse to follow his directions, he may chasten us for our disobedience. But it cannot be said that God's requirements are so unreasonable that none of us can keep them; we must not assert that all who are born of God have to be chastened for disobedience. There is one and only one kind of chastening "whereof all are partakers," which proves that a man is born of God, and the absence of which proves his profession of the new birth a mistake. That chastening amounts to an impulse and an urging on, to an experience known as holiness. The teaching of the passage is that all except nominal Christians are bound to experience that chastening. He says in the 8th verse, "If ye be without (this) chastisement, then are ye bastards and not sons;" that is, you are children of the church, but you are not children of God. The church is your mother, but God is not your father.

In the 11th verse he tells us that no chastening for the present seemeth to be joyous. In the words "no chastening" he refers to all those various kinds of chastisement to which we have alluded, showing that he recognizes more than one class of chastisement. Chastening may come with any degree of intensity, from the mildest correction to the severest scourging. But it never makes you happy, even if it be only a correction for mispronouncing a word. When corrected, you do not feel like shouting for joy. While it does not seem to be joyous, you may thank the individual for it, and number it among your valuable assets, because "afterwards it yieldeth the peaceable fruit of rightness." But it only yieldeth this fruit provided you are responsive; only "to them which are exercised thereby."

A Four-Cornered Fact

Four significant truths are enfolded in the words of Hebrews 12:10. First, that there is such a thing as Christian holiness. Second, that there is such a thing as a child of God not having it. Third, that this holiness is an experience. Fourth, that we may have it today.

We are gradually coming to that state of enlightenment where there are very few people who would deny the first of these four truths, that there is such a thing as Christian holiness. They sometimes attempt to generalize the subject and identify it with justification or with death or with purgatory; but they admit in some fashion that there is such a thing. The second truth, that there is such a thing as a child of God not having this holiness, can hardly be made plainer by an exposition of the verse under consideration. The apostle has just implied in verse 8 that all illegitimate professors of the new birth are dismissed from the discussion, that merely nominal Christians may not have this impulse to holiness. The spurious Christian is

SOUL PILOTS

known in that he does not feel this divine pull toward the higher grace. There is analogy between the earthly father and his child and the heavenly Father and His child. While even the careless observer may recognize the two first mentioned teachings of verse 10, the other two truths may seem elusive to the Bible reader. It should require little reflection, however, to see that the Father is urging His children, not to a mere improvement in behavior, not to an ever receding ideal, but to an experience of heart. In wishing that we become partakers of His holiness, he uses the same term that we commonly employ when we speak of enjoying Christmas dinner with a friend. "Partake." Therein is suggested a definite something, which God desires us to get in our souls; a something which looks towards qualification for better service; a something with enjoyable proportions, which, while rendering the believer more pleasing to God, brings profound pleasure to the believer. Nor would God chasten us today in view of something we should get tomorrow. If you chasten your child for the nonperformance of a duty, you do not chasten him until the day assigned for the performance of that duty. Then, when he has failed to meet the reasonable demand laid upon him, your chastening comes, which signifies to him that it is high time for him to be meeting your requirements. There is no intelligence in chastening a child in anticipation of some future order or requirement. We do not chasten them in order that they might grow. There are those who think that the attainment of Christian holiness is by a process of growth; but, while chastening may serve as an outward means to improve conduct, it would be a very strange thing for the Lord to employ chastening as a means to facilitate growth. Indeed growth is a putting on, while holiness, as regards the process of its attainment, is a putting off. He who introduces a long extended time element in the attainment of heart purity virtually teaches that it cannot be fully realized in this life, and that the chastenings of the Lord are meaningless. For, in the first place, no child of God has the guarantee of a long extension of time in which to grow; and, in the second place, the inequalities which place some at such great disadvantage as compared to others, in the period of growth allotted, would make it necessary to recognize a class of believers whom it would be unfair to chasten. Yet we are told that "all are partakers" of this chastening unto holiness. We conclude that Christian holiness is an experience, provided for the soul of the believer, and is due to be received any time after one becomes a child of God and an heir of the inheritance among them that are sanctified by faith. It is widely the experience of God's children that the Father begins to work on their soul, urging them and moving them toward the

SOUL PILOTS

fulness of the blessing, as soon as they have become His children and have communion with Him.

THE ISSUE ALL MUST FACE

You will notice that the holiness he desires us to obtain is *His* holiness. There may be some details about *my* picture of it that you do not like. Professed representatives may fail to illustrate it according to what you know is right. you may think that certain persons and movements present eccentricities aside from holiness that are unwarranted. You will be wise if you remember that our present treasures are in earthen vessels, that the highest ministry must come to us through frail men; but you are entirely free from responsibility if you reject my holiness or Mr. B——'s or Mr. C——'s holiness. You are not asked to accept John Wesley's holiness; you are only called upon to accept *His* holiness. If there are things about us that you do not like, you can discard those things without any fear of bad results, provided you do not at the same time lay down something that belongs to *His* holiness. We do not propose to complicate the issue upon this one great thing without which no man shall see the Lord. We do not presume to say you must accept holiness and "this" or "that" or us or another notion; we do not proclaim that all our program or the program of any other uninspired teacher of this truth must be accepted or rejected as a whole. You do not have to accept *us* at all. We are pretty sure of several other Scriptural truths which are not essential to the message of holiness. If they are truths, you will some day believe them, when the mists have rolled away and you see things as they are; but we shall not urge upon you the immediate acceptance of any statement except that which exalts Jesus Christ in his saving office and introduces you to God's best.

There should be no confusion of the issue; it is all right to reject foolishness, it may be all right to reject denominational shibboleths or to reject men who bring us a message; but you must be careful that the broom which sweeps these from the vestibule of your hospitality does not sweep out the promise of God. So long as the issue is between you and man you have an even chance; but we are told in 1 Thes. 4:7, 8, that he who rejects that holiness to which God calls us, rejects not man but God. That remarkable passage is addressed to Christians, as are all the Epistles. In it he has a double aim; one is to keep them from going down again, and the other is to get them to go up to higher things. He gives them to understand that they will have many downward impulses and downward pulls, but those drawings do not come from God; that God's call is not unto uncleanness but unto holiness. If they have any quarrel with reference to the convenience or desirableness of such a call, they are informed that the issue is not between them and any preacher, or movement, or church; but it is between them and God, and that drawing back means to reject not man but God "who has also given unto us the Holy Spirit." He would have us to understand that the gift of the Holy Spirit represents God's special provision to effect the work of holiness in the hearts of believers. That is a very important point of which, in passing, we may remind you; to remember the essential relation between holiness and the gift of the Holy Spirit would save us from following after that oft repeated mistake of supposing the New Testament experience of holiness is possible apart from or prior to the gift of the Holy Spirit. Men may make serious and offensive mistakes in telling us what God wants us to be and do, and they may fail to illustrate their message; they may be wide of the mark in prescribing for you certain modes of seeking, or certain visions and sensations, as a part of the Bible blessing; but they will not make any mistake in telling you that God requires the standard, and that every facility for its realization is provided in the gift of the Holy Ghost. They may safely stand aside and leave the issue between you and God; the responsibility is upon you. One of Satan's finest methods of keeping people out of this great blessing is to get them full of prejudice against some person or movement, and have them suppose that the rejection of the man frees them from any obligation to consider his message.

When the Chastening Ceases

The apostle says that "for a few days," for a short time, our earthly fathers chastened us; after a while, whether success or failure resulted from their efforts, they ceased. He is drawing an analogy. The inference, solemnly sustained elsewhere in the Scriptures and in the lives of men who have seen their day, the inference is, that God will finally cease to remind and urge, and let us alone on this subject. When a Christian thus becomes sophisticated and full of his own notions, and says, "I have no more interest in that subject, I do not have any drawings in that direction," his spiritual status becomes a problem. We find in him another reason for being thankful that the final judgment is to be resolved by the infinite Judge. But, we may say we should shudder to stand in the shoes of one who thus had disposed of the inward urgings of the Spirit and the chastenings of the Lord. Too often have men been responsive to this appeal in the more sensitive period of their spiritual history, and later, becoming fossilized, opposed the thing they had formerly sought, wishing that the world would forget the day when it was whispered, "He is at the altar for sanctification."

This holiness, being *His* holiness, is the most beautiful thing in the world. When the Psalmist contemplates and sings about it, he calls it the beauty of holiness, describing it as a feasible standard of worship. Holiness gets its beauty from our Lord Himself. All nature has been drawn upon for an illustration to set forth His beauty. He is called the rose of Sharon, the lily of the valley, the fairest among ten thousand. So glorious is He that He imparts glory to everything with which He is connected. And so beautiful is true Christian holiness that it is hard to make it repulsive to a discerning observer. People experienced in divine things get to where they will see through the rubbish of human nature and the follies of its ignorance and appreciate the beauty of holiness, notwithstanding. If we meet with those certain marks which indicate that people have submitted themselves to the sanctifying blood of Christ, we should be able to tolerate in them a great many human faults and imperfections, before turning away from them. Christian holiness is not a sectarian doctrine. It says of every one who receives the blood of Christ in personal cleansing, they are my people; whether their theology be Arminian or Calvinistic; whether their church government be Congregational, Presbyterian or Episcopalian; whatever be their form of baptism or apprehension of sacraments. The beauty of holiness renders transparent every disfiguring veneer and makes the life to shine. The most beautiful thing in all the world, it bids defiance to every ordinary obstruction, and lends comeliness to the humblest and homeliest of men. One of the fathers said it was so beautiful that no ordinary normal dog would bark at it or make an attack upon it unless you dressed it in a bear skin. Satan would like very much to put a bear skin upon this glorious New Testament experience, and start it through the streets of Tokyo with all the dogs assailing it. If he should succeed in doing this it would be "His holiness," just the same, and it would have our sympathies; but we ought not to permit the enemy to do this; we who stand for this work of God's grace, ought jealously to put forward its testimony in the very best form and to the best advantage possible, so that people may see it as it is, without the issue being complicated or the perspective obstructed.

X

VICTORY

BASED UPON GENESIS 32:24-31

"I will not let thee go except thou bless me."

THE experiences of the Old Testament patriarchs have about them a symbolic and prophetic significance. They are designed to point out and anticipate the experiences of the New Testament. There may be phases of difference in the spiritual attainments of the saints of the Old Testament and the saints of the New; but fundamentally there was much in common. Even the modes of entering a spiritual experience were illustrative. The ancients were under certain dispensational limitations; but, in spite of that, we may assume that a few men, such as Jacob, David, and Isaiah, walked so close with God that they reached all that is essential in the experience of full salvation as taught in the New Testament.

GOD DID NOT EVOLVE

The same God that is revealed in the New Testament is revealed in all parts of the Old;

the unchanging God. We simply learn more about Him with the progression of spiritual intelligence. The same salvation that is taught in the New Testament is taught in the Old, and on the same terms of consecration and faith. God tolerated some things in ancient times which He rebukes and will not tolerate today, but this does not mean that He compromised with them; He bore with those things until the world had learned the lesson which He meant to teach it. Referring to the olden time, St. Paul does not inform us that God had a different ideal; but he does inform us that God whom he represented was identical with God whom his fathers knew in the olden time, who in the times of men's ignorance winked at certain things that He now commands them to quit. There is no doubt that in the more ignorant ages of the world, when men knew almost nothing about God and His law, he found a way to save people that walked in all the light they had. We are not the judge of people who never heard of Bible holiness. We are not the judge of people who never heard of God or of Christ and His Gospel. We have a simple order to carry the message to them. But it has been true in every age, especially where God's revealed word was obtainable, that the possibilities of finding out the mysteries of salvation were almost unlimited. We have observed that in Old Testament times there were those who made such an aggressive

VICTORY

consecration and exercised such an implicit faith in God that they lived centuries ahead of their time, and partook of New Testament blessings. Because of their aggressiveness in meeting conditions God found an advance opportunity to show what He could do for a soul, to foreshow what He designed in the fulness of time to do upon a wide scale.

"GOD ALMIGHTY APPEARED UNTO ME"

Jacob was the twin brother of Esau, and, by divine appointment, was to become the heir of the estate and enjoy the blessings and privileges of the first born. But in his eagerness, he sought for the right thing the wrong way, and brought upon himself the anger of his rugged brother Esau. First, he found Esau hungry, and, taking advantage of the abnormal appetite and improvident spirit of his brother, he bought from Esau his birthright. Then, by the aid of his mother, with whom he was a favorite, he cheated Esau out of the patriarchial blessing. In the midst of this situation, when his life had been threatened by Esau, his mother used a pretext and induced his father to send him to her relatives in Mesopotamia, so she might save him from the wrath of his angry brother. In his lonely passage northward, he stopped to sleep at a place called Luz, which afterward was called Bethel, where he had that memorable vision of a ladder with angels ascending and descending upon it. In his solitude and sadness he turned to God, and entered into a covenant and built an altar, in imitation of his devout father and grandfather. "Surely," said he, "the Lord is in this place and I knew it not . . . this is none other but the house of God, and this is the gate of heaven." He there took God into partnership in all his temporal affairs; a thing which we are all to do if we would have the right foundation for our religious superstructure. The perpetual sign of this partnership was that he should give God a tenth of every thing he gained in the future. He went away into that strange land and spent more than twenty years, becoming the head of a large family, and quite rich in personal property. Our lesson finds him on his way back to his fatherland, to take his inheritance. He has sent a committee down to treat with his brother Esau and find out his temper, and the committee has returned to say that Esau had not recovered from his hostility during all those years, but was coming to meet Jacob with four hundred men.

A Lesson in the Valley

In a new and deeper sense, Jacob is suddenly brought to feel his utter dependence upon God for help; and this feeling, with the prayers which are to follow from it, is about to lead him to the discovery of his need of a deeper unity with God than he has ever had before. God has to bring us all into a crisis that we might see ourselves and the deeper needs of our souls. It developed in the interview which Jacob was to have with God that night, that he had inherited a nature, which accounted for his name, from which he was to have deliverance, as a condition to having power with God and with man. What he knew about original sin prior to that time we are not able to say; but it is probable that he had some sound views thereafter. Personal experience often leads a man to a doctrinal discovery. There are a good many brethren who claim the Lord as their God and have made a covenant with Him, who, failing to arrive at this deeper self discovery with its resultant inner cleansing, have not made the corresponding doctrinal discovery.

Before God can bring us to that deeper unity with Himself there must be somewhere along the way a crisis, usually brought on by Him, but which may and ought to be brought on by us. When we see our inner depravity we should array ourselves against it, and seek its destruction by the grace of God. I know a good many men in the States, and one who does not live far from my home, who had to come into serious crises and be visited with sore visitations before they could be brought into deeper unity with God. Some men of God have passed through deep valleys of affliction or severe persecutions, to come out endued with peculiar spiritual power. Out of this grew the idea with some of the ancients that there was a mysterious power in affliction and suffering to sanctify the soul. The plain explanation is, that in that condition the servant of God found himself and found his deeper need, a need which God cannot supply until the individual discovers and admits it. A man may do both at the same time, or he may make the discovery at one time and admit it later. If he is late making the discovery he will be late receiving the full blessing; if he is later admitting or confessing it, he will be later receiving the fulness.

God met Jacob in this hour of crisis, caused him to see the depravity of his soul, and he, meeting the conditions, laid hold upon the fulness of the blessing. Allowing for dispensational limitations, we may safely assume that when Paul speaks of "the fulness of the blessing of the gospel of Christ" he uses the word blessing with a meaning quite similar to that with which Jacob was moved to use it in his prayer for the blessing on his night of wrestling. The fulness of the blessing does not lay hold on you till you lay hold on it. Men do not wander along at leisure and stroll down some flowery pathway into full salvation. They go after it with tremendous earnestness before any ever get it.

The slothful man may look into this profound victory of the soul, with all the blessing that attends it, and wish he had it; but it is not for the slothful man.

Arriving at "Number One"

The account of Jacob's steps by which he approached this culmination in his inner life is symbolic of the stages through which the believer approaches the sanctification of his soul. Perhaps he did not know in advance all that would happen to him that night, but he had a strange conviction that there was to be a deeper union and a better understanding between himself and Jehovah. The circumstances of his life had furnished an occasion of affliction and turmoil, and he was going alone to pray over the *circumstances* of his life. He made his preliminary arrangements for this prayer by planning to send his possessions and his loved ones across the brook Jabbok, beginning with the inferior and ending with the one he loved best. First, he put across his flocks and herds, then the members of his family of whom he thought least, until he had separated from all but the dearest idol of his heart, his wife Rachel. This is usually the way people make their consecration. They give up the cheap things first, and then, lastly, the things which they prize most. Sometimes they stick there, and, cherishing some lingering idol, wonder why they do not get the blessing. But Jacob went further. He sent his beloved Rachel across the brook and went alone to pray. A man must get to where he can take the lone way, waiting for no one else to go, before he is an available subject to receive the fulness. But this does not mean that Jacob had passed all his difficulties. There still remained one obstacle in his way, and that was himself; old number one. This is the most stubborn proposition any of us have to deal with. A man's own old nature makes his life miserable when it is calculated to be full of sunshine and peace. Sometimes he will feel that all his family are mean and everything is gone wrong, when the explanation is that he is wrong. A drunken man stood in the door of a church, looking at the preacher and people, and said, "I never saw so many drunken people in my life." His own condition had colored his view of his surroundings. A certain man of the world who had just been saved and gone home said that his first impression was that there had been a great change for the better in his wife and children, and that all his domestic animals had found a religious experience. This truth that there is a natural law which causes a man's condition to color his surroundings seems to have taken deeper hold on Jacob as he continued in prayer; for though he began to offer a fervent prayer over his circumstances, he soon lost his

VICTORY

enthusiasm on this subject, and came to feel that everything depended on his receiving the personal blessing that the Lord had for him.

A Passion to Be Made Whole

A yet unread volume of suggestion exists in this unique way in which Jehovah manifested himself to the patriarch Jacob, and the strenuous treatment given him. It appears that the event was designed as a special lesson for seekers in the ages to come. The strange visitor first succeeded in leading Jacob to the true theory of peace—heart peace; then to the secret of real victory—by way of the throne; then to the ground work of full salvation—confess and get rid of the depraved self life. It was not possible to give Jacob the full blessing until his desire for it commanded the uppermost place in his heart and the larger part of his horizon. He must therefore pray on, and not be shown the final step, until this desire outstripped all other desires and laid them low beneath its feet. It was not possible for the Lord to give Jacob the blessing which he was seeking so long as Jacob could get along without it. The blessing of full salvation is not ready for a man who merely entertains a mild interest in a better experience; it is for him who cannot get along without it. If you see some way to make out without having this full will of God wrought in you it will be your privilege to continue without the blessing. When Jacob said, "I will not let thee go except thou bless me," he had reshaped his scale of values and reached a critical point in his resolution. It was equivalent to saying, I will die or have it; my future is involved in it and I cannot get along without it. This blessing is for all who cannot get along without it, and for them only. Men may *profess* full salvation with whom the desire for full salvation has never been supreme; but men cannot enter into the divine fulness till that desire becomes supreme. If an angel should hold this gift of God in one hand and a million yen or the crown of a kingdom in the other, offering you your choice, you would not be fit for the full blessing if your desire were not big enough to shove the earthly thing aside without hesitancy.

In the sermon on the mount the Master simplified the conditions of full salvation, the sole condition being that you must want it: "Blessed are they which do hunger and thirst." But, before God can do the work, the want must be one which knows no compromise, which accepts no substitute satisfaction, and which has no second choice. There is a law in the plan of salvation by which God must wait till one is ready for the fulness of the blessing before he can impart it; and they do not get ready by the addition of time, or by an increase of education, or by a growth of judgment, beyond that elementary judgment which recognizes our need and God's supply. They get ready by a growth of well defined, intelligent desire. This desire asserted itself in Jacob and rose to its full magnitude during that night of interview and prayer.

Incorporate the Blessing

The language of Jacob, "except thou bless me," sounds a little indefinite, as if he did not know exactly what he wanted. He may not have known all that was involved in it, but he knew pretty definitely what he wanted. We may assume that the prayer is greatly abridged; no doubt there were many words uttered that night which were not reduced to record; but we may be sure that there was a pretty good understanding between Jacob and Jehovah, for it takes definite prayer to get definite results, and there were definite results on this occasion. Whatever your terminology, or the words employed when you seek, they must have a definite meaning before you can exercise that definite faith which enables God to do a definite work in your heart. People who come to revival meetings and conventions and get "a great uplift" in an indefinite way, never have anything that lasts and bears fruit, to take away with them. The works of divine grace are expressed in promises and presented in doctrinal form in the Scriptures, and we should clearly apprehend those truths. They are the surest medium through which the blessing may come to the heart, and the adequate means of incorporating it when it does come. Unincorporated blessings vanish. Philosophers tell us that we cannot hold an idea without some term to correspond with it in our mind. Our words are symbols, and we cannot think without symbols. So, the doctrines of justification and sanctification or the baptism with the Holy Spirit, along with other truths which relate to God's dealing with the soul, are symbols of corresponding facts due to take place in us. Granting that men may hold the shell and miss the kernel, we must insist that those who enter intelligently upon their inheritance in Christ should be discriminating students of the symbols, taking definite ground in their doctrinal attitudes. If a man forgets the term through which God blessed him he is liable to forget the blessing.

Our Doctrinal Growing Point

Along toward morning, when Jacob asserted his determination to die or get what he came after, the Lord asked him his name. Then he asked Jehovah his name, but the Lord gave him to understand that there was nothing practical in that question on Jacob's part, no reason for it: "Wherefore (for what reason) is it that thou dost ask after my name?" which was as much as to say there was a reason in asking Jacob to confess his name. Herein, Jacob was brought to the final test of confessing the fact of his inherited nature, which gave him his name. It would appear that his name was given by inspiration, for it designated something in his nature which could be discerned only by divine insight. The consequence of "the blessing" is expressly stated by the divine wrestler; endued with power, and changed in nature, from supplanter to prince: "As a prince hast thou power with God and with men, and hast prevailed." He prevailed, first, with God; then, as a consequence, with men. But before Jacob could get that power which put him up, he had to put himself down, in a confession that there was something in his nature which needed to be taken out. To go up, spiritually, there must be a going down. That is where the test comes; that is where a great many important brethren quit praying and let the Wrestler go. We do not like to call ourselves bad names. We do not like to discover something in ourselves that ought not to be there. There is a doctrinal tenet that says a man can be endued with power without reference to cleansing; but he can not. Let us set the answer to that error in bold relief: *He can not*. God can not trust him with it. A man whom God cannot cleanse he cannot trust with an enduement of power. Such a man may get his imagination endued, he may fly off into a volume of good feeling and suppose he has struck the blessing; but no man has ever reached the real enduement of power until he has struck bottom in the confession of inbred sin. So long as he holds on to his own foolish negations God cannot fill him or give him the victory in the battle of life, but must permit him to go on in failure and defeat. If Esau meets such a man he will usually defeat the man. The only way that man will be able to go on is never to meet Esau with his four hundred men.

Multiplying a Man

But Jacob was not a quitter, and he proved not to be an evader. He was a man who could learn by experience. Coming against facts, he called them by their right name, and did not try to call them something else. He did not fall back on his philosophy or his theology, or adhere to a prejudice fostered in some circle of abstract speculators. And the very moment God got him to where he would let Him have His way with him, that moment God took his embarrassing name away from him and gave him a good name. Jacob had fought it out that night in the shadows until his desire had become stronger than his flesh, and in his wrestling he had disjointed his limb. God had been patiently dealing with him ever since he was a boy. No doubt he had been a problem to his neighbors and kinsmen and parents, so perverse and so subtle was he by nature. Many times they may have prophesied that Jacob would come to no good end; but, buried under all the rubbish of his natural depravity, God saw that magnificent man who was to stand out in the annals of history for having excelled at the throne of grace. God held on to Jacob and Jacob held on to God, through the years, until the crisis came at Peniel. Jacob had fibre enough for God to lay hold of him, and had in his heart the elements of ultimate response. If he had not drawn the line on his old self life and fought it out, going on to complete victory, you would scarcely have heard of him today. We have people today in whose favor their neighbors cannot say much, but in whom God can see something, and if He could lead them to seek deliverance from their old depraved nature, He could give them an influence which this whole Empire would be too small to contain. He would be pleased to do this for many who today are not known or felt beyond their local community, and whose influence is of uncertain flavor, even in its small radius. Many well meaning people, reasonably devout, with vast possibilities buried in their faculties, are passing through life to the graveyard and the judgment, unknown and unfelt, simply because they have not drawn the issue against their depraved nature and found their Peniel victory, which, in more modern terms, would be called their pentecost.

Jacob went from the hillside that morning, mighty in God, representing an advanced standard. He was never to be the same again. There was a fascinating influence in his life, ever afterward. After that, he always took sides with God, even though it should be against his own family or against himself. Loyalty to God was to characterize all his deportment. And, as Jacob prevailed with God, something had happened to Esau; and something will happen to every man that gets across the track of a man like that. We do not know when that something happened to Esau; I rather think it happened when he met Jacob. As the rugged Esau approached his newly blessed brother there came over him the feeling, I cannot hit that man. There seemed to be a power in Israel's presence that day which melted the heart of Esau. It is very hard to hit a man who has prayed all night. Surrounding the person of a man who comes from the throne of grace, victorious over self and cleansed from sin, is an atmosphere in which the enemy loses his liberty to strike.

THE EVENING HALO

As Jacob had let God have his way with him, God honored Jacob in all his subsequent days.

VICTORY

In his old age, when he was blessing his sons, he refers to the two great meetings which he had with God. Record of this is left us in the forty-eighth of Genesis. In the third verse, he says: "God Almighty appeared unto me at Luz in the land of Canaan and blessed me." It was a lingering blessing, an epochal blessing, which he had never forgotten. It represented a principal milestone in his life. Then in the sixteenth verse, the dying patriarch records the event which we are studying today, where he insistently demanded a blessing of Him who had blessed him at Bethel. Here he refers to Jehovah as "the angel which redeemed me from all evil." There may be superficial observers who think that the greatest evil that God redeemed him from at Peniel on the night of wrestling was the threatened fate he was to meet next day. But the greatest evil God delivered him from was that heritage of his nature which went with the passing of his old name, and the passing of which made him a prince, duly qualified in spirit and life to represent the King. And, in his dying moments, God gave signal honor to His aged servant; pulling back the curtains of the future, He permitted him to see the glories of the New Testament age, and said to him: "The scepter shall not depart from Judah, nor a lawgiver from between his feet, until Shiloh come; and unto him shall the gathering of the people be." And so the man who so early partook of the first essentials of full salvation was led to a prophetic Pisgah in his dying hour, and given to see the ingathering of the nations which should result from the influence of Judah's greatest Son, whose redeeming power was to be made known in the ends of the earth by witnesses filled with the Holy Ghost.

THE LIFE OF CHRIST

P. WHITWELL WILSON   *of the London Daily News*

The Christ We Forget

A Life of Our Lord for Men of To-day. 8vo, cloth, net $1.50.

A book with scarcely a peer in contemporary publishing. The author, an English University man, brilliant journalist, and sometime member of Parliament, writes the story of Jesus of Nazareth in a wonderfully arresting fashion. His book is utterly free from theological terminology or conventional viewpoint presenting a picture of Jesus which while actually new is astonishingly convincing.

EDGAR YOUNG MULLINS, D.D.   *Pres. Southern Baptist Theo'l Sem., Louisville*

The Life in Christ   Net $1.25.

"Dr. Mullins has recognition throughout the country as a great teacher. This volume shows him a preacher of intellectual and spiritual power. Excellent models for the growing minister, forcible, intellectual, spiritual."—*Christian Advocate.*

FRANCIS E. CLARK, D.D.   *President United Society Christian Endeavor*

Christ and the Young People

12mo, cloth, net 50c.

"A study of the Life of Jesus in a quite unusual vein. The editor has seldom during his life been so helped by the printed page. It is indeed a remarkable presentation of the life of Jesus, sincere and impartial."—*Zion's Herald.*

JAMES M. GRAY, D.D.   *Dean Moody Bible Institute*

A Picture of the Resurrection

12mo, boards, net 35c.

A plain, unadorned examination of the historical fact of Our Lord's Resurrection, of its indispensable prominence in the faith of the Christian and of the power its acceptance exercises in buttressing his belief in a physical resurrection from the dead, and the attainment of life eternal.

A. T. ROBERTSON, M.A., D.D.

The Divinity of Christ in the Gospel of John   12mo, cloth, net $1.00.

"A fascinating study of the Gospel of John. The book is not a full commentary on the Gospel, but an effort to develop the thesis of the book with brevity and clearness, so that the average man may understand the book better as a whole in detail."—*Christian Observer.*

PULPIT AND PEW

PROF. WILLIAM J. HUTCHINS   *The Oberlin Graduate School of Theology*
The Preacher's Ideals and Inspirations
George Shepherd Foundation Lectures. Net $1.00.

"Professor Hutchins' work with his students, out of which these lectures have grown, has been so stimulating and enlightening, that I rejoice that the fruit of his long thinking on the Preacher's problem is to be made available to others also."—*Pres. Henry Churchill King,* of Oberlin.

ELIJAH P. BROWN (Ram's Horn)   *Author of "The Real Billy Sunday"*
Point and Purpose in Preaching
12mo, cloth, net $1.00.

"Dr. Brown is perhaps best known as the *Ram's Horn Man,* having been for a long while editor of *The Ham's Horn,* which under his administration was a power for good. Good reading for us all, but it is of special value to ministers."
—*Herald of Gospel Liberty.*

ALBERT F. McGARRAH   *Author of "Modern Church Finance"*
Modern Church Management
12mo, cloth, net $1.00.

With thoroughness and constructive ability, Mr. McGarrah furnishes valuable advice concerning the ideals and policies of the modern church and what she may learn and profit by, from a study of the principles of scientific management.

JOHN F. COWAN, D.D.
Big Jobs for Little Churches
12mo, cloth, net 75c.

Deals with the manifold problems confronting the rural church in an optimistic, constructive sort of way. Furnishes helpful, suggestive plans of work and methods of procedure which have been found to yield highly satisfactory results.

JOSEPH FORT NEWTON   *Pastor City Temple, London*
An Ambassador
City Temple Sermons. 12mo, cloth, net $1.00.

"Most of the sermons were preached by Dr. Newton in the City Temple, London. Dr. Newton has both vigor of thought and an unusual felicity of expression. And it is good, earnest gospel preaching as well."—*Christian Guardian.*

HUGH THOMPSON KERR, D.D.
The Highway of Life
12mo, cloth, net $1.00.

Dr. Kerr has long established himself as a man with a message. Some of his fine pulpit efforts are here presented, furnishing ample evidence that this talented preacher has something to say of an enheartening character.

www.ingramcontent.com/pod-product-compliance
Lightning Source LLC
Chambersburg PA
CBHW031349040426
42444CB00005B/244